A HANDY GUIDE FOR BEGGARS

ESPECIALLY THOSE OF THE POETIC FRATERNITY

Being sundry explorations, made while afoot and penniless in Florida, Georgia, North Carolina, Tennessee, Kentucky, New Jersey, and Pennsylvania. These adventures convey and illustrate the rules of beggary for poets and some others

By VACHEL LINDSAY

Author of "The Congo," "The Art of The Moving Picture," "Adventures while Preaching the Gospel of Beauty," etc.

THE MACMILLAN COMPANY

PUBLISHERS   MCMXVI

Norwood Press
J. S. Cushing Co. — Berwick & Smith Co.
Norwood, Mass., U.S.A.

Karl H Carlson
- 1917 -

A HANDY GUIDE FOR BEGGARS

THE MACMILLAN COMPANY
NEW YORK · BOSTON · CHICAGO · DALLAS
ATLANTA · SAN FRANCISCO

MACMILLAN & CO., Limited
LONDON · BOMBAY · CALCUTTA
MELBOURNE

THE MACMILLAN CO. OF CANADA, Ltd.
TORONTO

ACKNOWLEDGEMENTS

THE author desires to express his indebtedness to *The Outlook* for permission to reprint the adventures in the South and to Charles Zueblin for permission to reprint the adventures in the East.

The author desires to express his indebtedness to the *Chicago Herald* for permission to reprint *The Would-be Merman*, and to *The Forum* for *What the Sexton Said*, and to *The Yale Review* for *The Tramp's Refusal*.

The author wishes to express his gratitude to Mr. George Mather Richards, Miss Susan Wilcox, Mr. and Mrs. Frank Ide and Miss Grace Humphrey for their generous help and advice in preparing this work.

DEDICATION AND PREFACE OF A HANDY GUIDE FOR BEGGARS

THERE are one hundred new poets in the villages of the land. This Handy Guide is dedicated first of all *to them*.

It is also dedicated to the younger sons of the wide earth, to the runaway boys and girls getting further from home every hour, to the prodigals who are still wasting their substance in riotous living, be they gamblers or blasphemers or plain drunks; to those heretics of whatever school to whom life is a rebellion with banners; to those who are willing to accept counsel if it be mad counsel.

This book is also dedicated to those budding philosophers who realize that every creature is a beggar in the presence of the beneficent sun, to those righteous ones who know that all righteousness is as filthy rags.

Moreover, as an act of contrition, reënlistment and fellowship this book is dedicated to all the children of Don Quixote who see giants where most folks see windmills: those Galahads dear to Christ and those virgin sisters of Joan of Arc who serve the lepers on their knees and march in shabby armor against the proud, who look into the lightning with the eyes of the mountain cat. They do more soldierly things every day than this book records, yet they are mine own people, my nobler kin to whom I have been recreant, and so I finally dedicate this book *to them*.

These are the rules of the road : —

(1) Keep away from the Cities;

(2) Keep away from the railroads;

(3) Have nothing to do with money and carry no baggage;

(4) Ask for dinner about quarter after eleven;

(5) Ask for supper, lodging and breakfast about quarter of five;

(6) Travel alone;

(7) Be neat, deliberate, chaste and civil;

(8) Preach the Gospel of Beauty.

And without further parley, let us proceed to inculcate these, by illustration, precept and dogma.

VACHEL LINDSAY.

Springfield, Illinois,
November, 1916.

TABLE OF CONTENTS

FOLLOW THE THISTLEDOWN

I asked her "Is Aladdin's Lamp
Hidden anywhere?"
"Look into your heart," she said,
"Aladdin's Lamp is there."

She took my heart with glowing hands.
It burned to dust and air
And smoke and rolling thistledown,
Blowing everywhere.

"Follow the thistledown," she said,
"Till doomsday if you dare,
Over the hills and far away.
Aladdin's Lamp is there."

I

VAGRANT ADVENTURES IN THE SOUTH

COLUMBUS

Would that we had the fortunes of Columbus.
Sailing his caravels a trackless way,
He found a Universe — he sought Cathay.
God give such dawns as when, his venture o'er,
The Sailor looked upon San Salvador.
God lead us past the setting of the sun
To wizard islands, of august surprise;
God make our blunders wise.

THE MAN UNDER THE YOKE

It was Sunday morning in the middle of March. I was stranded in Jacksonville, Florida. After breakfast I had five cents left. Joyously I purchased a sack of peanuts, then started northwest on the railway ties straight toward that part of Georgia marked "Swamp" on the map.

Sunset found me in a pine forest. I decided to ask for a meal and lodging at the white house looming half a mile ahead just by the track. I prepared a speech to this effect:—

"I am the peddler of dreams. I am the sole active member of the ancient brotherhood of the troubadours. It is against the rules of our order to receive money. We have the habit of asking a night's lodging in exchange for repeating verses and fairy tales."

As I approached the house I forgot the speech. All the turkeys gobbled at me fiercely. The two dogs almost tore down the fence trying to get a taste of me. I went to the side

gate to appeal to the proud old lady crowned
with a lace cap and enthroned in the porch
rocker. Her son, the proprietor, appeared.
He shall ever be named the dog-man. His
tone of voice was such, that, to speak in meta-
phor, he bit me in the throat. He refused
me a place in his white kennel. He would
not share his dog-biscuit. The being on the
porch assured me in a whanging yelp that
they did not take "nobody in under no cir-
cumstances." Then the dog-man, mollified by
my serene grin, pointed with his thumb into
the woods, saying: "There is a man in there
who will take you in sure." He said it as
though it were a reflection on his neighbor's
dignity. That I might not seem to be hurrying, I asked if his friend kept watch-dogs.
He assured me the neighbor could not afford
them.

The night with the man around the corner
was like a chapter from that curious document,
"The Gospel according to St. John." He
"could not afford to turn a man away" because once he slept three nights in the rain
when he walked here from west Georgia. No
one would give him shelter. After that he

decided that when he had a roof he would go shares with whoever asked. Some strangers were good, some bad, but he would risk them all. Imagine this amplified in the drawling wheeze of the cracker sucking his corn-cob pipe for emphasis.

His real name and address are of no consequence. I found later that there were thousands like him. But let us call him "The Man Under the Yoke." He was lean as an old opium-smoker. He was sooty as a pair of tongs. His Egyptian-mummy jaws had a two-weeks' beard. His shirt had not been washed since the flood. His ankles were innocent of socks. His hat had no band. I verily believe his pipe was hereditary, smoked first by a bond-slave in Jamestown, Virginia.

He could not read. I presume his wife could not. They were much embarrassed when I wanted them to show me Lakeland on the map. They had warned me against that village as a place where itinerant strangers were shot full of holes. Well, I found that town pretty soon on the map, and made the brief, snappy memorandum in my notebook: "Avoid Lakeland."

There were three uncertain chairs on the porch, one a broken rocker. Therefore the company sat on the railing, loafing against the pillars. The plump wife was frozen with diffidence. The genial, stubby neighbor, a man from away back in the woods, after telling me how to hop freight-cars, departed through an aperture in the wandering fence.

The two babies on the floor, squealing like shoats, succeeded in being good without being clean. They wrestled with the puppies who emerged from somewhere to the number of four. I wondered if the Man Under the Yoke would turn to a dog-man when the puppies grew up and learned to bark.

Supper was announced with the admonition, "Bring the chairs." The rocking chair would not fit the kitchen table. Therefore the two babies occupied one, and the lord of the house another, and the kitchen chair was allotted to your servant. The mother hastened to explain that she was "not hungry." After snuffing the smoking lamp that had no chimney, she paced at regular intervals between the stove and her lord, piling hot biscuits before him.

I could not offer my chair, and make it plain that some one must stand. I expressed my regrets at her lack of appetite and fell to. Their hospitality did not fade in my eyes when I considered that they ate such provisions every day. There was a dish of salt pork that tasted like a salt mine. We had one deep plate in common containing a soup of luke-warm water, tallow, half-raw fat pork and wilted greens. This dish was innocent of any enhancing condiment. I turned to the biscuit pile.

They were raw in the middle. I kept up courage by watching the children consume the tallow soup with zest. After taking one biscuit for meat, and one for vegetables, I ate a third for good-fellowship. The mother was anxious that her children should be a credit, and shook them too sternly and energetically I thought, when they buried their hands in the main dish.

Meanwhile the Man Under the Yoke told me how his bosses in the lumber-camp kept his wages down to the point where the grocery bill took all his pay; how he was forced to trade at the "company" store, there in the heart of the pine woods. He had cut himself in the saw-pit, had been laid up for a month, and "like a fool" had gone back to the same business. Last year he had saved a little money, expecting to get things "fixed up nice," but the whole family was sick from June till October. He liked his fellow-workmen. They had to stand all he did. They loved the woods, and because of this love would not move to happier fortunes. Few had gone farther than Jacksonville. They did not understand travelling. They did not understand the traveller and were "likely to be mean to him." Then he asked me whether I thought "niggers" had souls. I answered "Yes." He agreed reluctantly. "They have a soul, of course, but it's a mighty small one." We adjourned to the front room, carrying our chairs down a corridor, where the open doorways we passed displayed uncarpeted floors and no furniture. The echo of the slow steps of the Man Under the Yoke reverberated through the wide house like muffled drums at a giant's funeral. Yet the largeness of the empty house was wealth. I have been entertained since in many a poorer castle;

for instance, in Tennessee, where a deaf old man, a crone, and her sister, a lame man, a slug of a girl, and a little unexplained boy ate, cooked, and slept by an open fire. They had neither stove, lamp, nor candle. I was made sacredly welcome for the night, though it was a one-room cabin with a low roof and a narrow door.

Thanks to the Giver of every good and perfect gift, pine-knots cost nothing in a pine forest. New York has no such fireplaces as that in the front room of the Man Under the Yoke. I thought of an essay by a New England sage on compensation. There were many old scriptures rising in my heart as I looked into that blaze. The one I remembered most was "I was a stranger, and ye took me in." But though it was Sunday night, I did not quote Scripture to my host.

It was seven o'clock. The wife had put her babies to bed. She sat on the opposite side of the fire from us. Eight o'clock was bedtime, the host had to go to work so early. But our three hearts were bright as the burning pine for an hour.

You have enjoyed the golden embossed

brocades of Hokusai. You have felt the
charm of Maeterlinck's "The Blind." Think
of these, then think of the shoulders of the
Man Under the Yoke, embossed by the flame.
Think of his voice as an occult instrument,
while he burned a bit of crackling brush, and
spoke of the love he bore that fireplace, the
memory of evenings his neighbors had spent
there with him, the stories told, the pipes
smoked, the good silent times with wife and
children. It was said by hints, and repeti-
tions, and broken syllables, but it was said.
We ate and drank in the land of heart's desire.
This man and his wife sighed at the fitting
times, and smiled, when to smile was to understand, while I recited a few of the rhymes of
the dear singers of yesterday and to-day:
Yeats and Lanier, Burns and even Milton.
This fire was the treasure at the end of the
rainbow. I had not been rainbow-chasing in
vain.

As my host rose and knocked out his pipe,
he told how interesting lumbering with oxen
could be made, if a man once understood
how they were driven. He assured me that
the most striking thing in all these woods

was a team of ten oxen. He directed me to a road whereby I would be sure to see half a dozen to-morrow. He said if ever I met a literary man, to have him write them into verses. Therefore the next day I took the route and observed: and be sure, if ever I meet the proper minstrel, I shall exhort him with all my strength to write the poem of the yoke.

As to that night, I slept in that room in the corner away from the fireplace. One comfort was over me, one comfort and pillow between me and the dark floor. The pillow was laundered at the same time as the shirt of my host. There was every reason to infer that the pillow and comfort came from his bed.

They slept far away, in some mysterious part of the empty house. I hoped they were not cold. I looked into the rejoicing fire. I said: "This is what I came out into the wilderness to see. This man had nothing, and gave me half of it, and we both had abundance."

THE MAN WITH THE APPLE–GREEN EYES

Remember, if you go a-wandering, the road will break your heart. It is sometimes like a woman, caressing and stabbing at once. It is a mystery, this quality of the road. I write, not to explain, but to warn, and to give the treatment. Comradeship and hospitality are opiates most often at hand.

I remember when I encountered the out-poured welcome of an Old Testament Patriarch, a praying section boss in a gray log village, one Monday evening in north Florida. He looked at me long. He sensed my depression. He made me his seventh son.

He sent his family about to announce my lecture in the schoolhouse on "The Value of Poetry." Enough apple-cheeked maidens, sad mothers, and wriggling, large-eyed urchins assembled to give an unconscious demonstration of the theme.

The little lamp spluttered. The windows

rattled. Two babies cried. Everybody assumed that lectures were delightful, miserable, and important. The woman on the back seat nursed her baby, reducing the noise one third. When I was through shouting, they passed the hat. I felt sure I had carried my point. Poetry was eighty-three cents valuable, a good deal for that place. And the sons of the Patriarch were the main contributors, for before the event he had thunderously exhorted them to be generous. I should not have taken the money? But that was before I had a good grip on my rule.

The Patriarch was kept away by a neighbor who had been seized with fits on Sunday, while fishing. The neighbor though mending physically, was in a state of apprehension. He demanded, with strong crying and tears, that the Patriarch pray with him. Late in the evening, as we were about the hearth, recovering from the lecture, my host returned from the sinner's bed, the pride of priesthood in his step. He had established a contrite heart in his brother, though all the while frank with him about the doubtful efficacy of prayer in healing a body visited with just wrath.

Who would not have loved the six sons, when, at the Patriarch's command, they drew into a circle around the family altar, with their small sister, and the gentle mother with her babe at her breast? It was an achievement to put the look of prayer into such flushed, wilful faces as those boys displayed. They followed their father with the devotion of an Ironside regiment as he lifted up his voice singing "The Son of God goes forth to War." They rolled out other strenuous hymns. I thought they would sing through the book. I looked at the mother. I thanked God for her. She was the only woman in Florida who could cook. And her voice was honey. Her breast was ivory. The child was a pearl. Her whole aspect had the age and the youth of one of De Forest Brush's austere American madonnas. The scripture lesson, selected not by chance, covered the adventures of Jacob at Bethel.

We afterwards knelt on the pine floor, our heads in the seats of the chairs. I peeped and observed the Patriarch with his chair almost in the fireplace. He ignored the heat. He shouted the name of the smallest boy, who answered the roll-call by praying: "Now I

lay me down to sleep." The father mega-
phoned for the next, and the next, with a like
response. He called the girl's name, but in
a still small voice she lisped the Lord's Prayer.
As the older boys were reached, the prayers
became individual, but containing fragments
of "Now I lay me." The mother petitioned
for the soul of the youngest boy, not yet in a
state of grace, for a sick cousin, and many a
neighborhood cause. The father prayed twenty
minutes, while the chair smoked. I forgot the
chair at last when he voiced the petition that
the stranger in the gates might have visitations
on his lonely road, like Jacob at Bethel. Then
a great appeal went up the chimney that the
whole assembly might bear abundantly the
fruits of the spirit. The fire leaped for joy.
I knew that when the prayer appeared before
the throne, it was still a tongue of flame.

* * * * * * *

Next morning I spent about seventy cents
lecture money on a railway ticket, and tried
to sleep past my destination, but the conductor woke me. He put me off in the Oke-
fenokee swamp, just inside the Georgia line.
The waters had more brass-bespangled ooze

c

than in mid-Florida; the marsh weeds beneath were lustrous red. I crossed an interminable trestle over the Suwannee River. A fidgety bird was scolding from tie to tie. If the sky had been turned over and the azure boiled to a spoonful, you would have had the intense blue with which he was painted. If the caldron had been filled with sad clouds, and boiled to a black lump, you would have had my heart. Ungrateful, I had forgotten the Patriarch. I was lonely for I knew not what; maybe for my friend Edward Broderick, who had walked with me through central Florida, and had been called to New York by the industrial tyranny which the steel rails represented even here.

We two had taken the path beside the railway in the regions of Sanford and Tampa, walking in loose sand white as salt. An orange grove in twilight had been a sky of little moons. We had eaten not many oranges. They are expensive there. But we had stolen the souls of all we passed, and so had spoiled them for their owners. It had been an exquisite revenge.

We had seen swamps of parched palmettos

set afire by wood-burning locomotives whose volcanic smoke-stacks are squat and wide, like those on the engines in grandmother's third reader.

We had met Mr. Terrapin, Mr. Owl, Mrs. Cow, and Master Calf, all of them carved by the train-wheels, Mr. Buzzard sighing beside them. We had met Mr. Pig again at the cracker's table, cooked by last year's forest-fire, run over by last year's train. But what had it mattered? For we together had had ears for the mocking-bird, and eyes for the moss-hung live oaks that mourn above the brown swamp waters.

We had met few men afoot, only two professional tramps, yet the path by the railway was clearly marked. Some Florida poet must celebrate the Roman directness of the railways embanked six feet above the swamp, going everywhere in regions that have no wagon-roads.

But wherever in our land there is a railway, there is a little path clinging to the embankment holding the United States in a network as real as that of the rolled steel, — a path wrought by the foot of the unsubdued. This path wanders back through history till it encounters Tramp Columbus, Tramp Dante, Tramp St. Francis, Tramp Buddha, and the rest of our masters.

All this we talked of nobly, even grandiloquently, but now I walked alone, ignoring the beautiful turpentine forests of Georgia and the sometime accepted merits of a quest for the Grail, the Gleam, or the Dark Tower. Reaching Fargo about one o'clock I attempted to telegraph for money to take me home, beaten. It was not a money-order office, and thirteen cents would not have covered the necessary business details. Forced to make the best of things, I spent all upon ginger-snaps at the combination grocery-store and railway-station. I shared them with a drummer waiting for the freight, who had the figure of Falstaff, and the mustaches of Napoleon third. I did not realize at that time, that by getting myself penniless I was inviting good luck.

After a dreary while, the local freight going to Valdosta came in. Napoleon advanced to capture a ride. A conductor and an inspector were on the platform. He attacked them with cigars. He indulged freely in friendly swearing and slapping on the back. He showed credentials, printed and written. He did not want to wait three hours for the passenger train in that much-to-be-condemned town. His cigars were refused, his papers returned. He took the path to the lumberman's hotel. His defeat appeared to be the inspector's doing.

That obstinate inspector wore a gray stubble beard and a collar chewed by many laundries. He was encompassed in a black garment of state that can be described as a temperance overcoat. He needed only a bulging umbrella and a nose like a pump-spout to resemble the caricatures of the Prohibition Party that appeared in *Puck* when St. John ran for President.

I showed him all my baggage carried in an oil-cloth wrapper in my breast pocket: a blue bandanna, a comb, a little shaving mirror, a tooth-brush, a razor, and a piece of soap. "These," I said, "are my credentials."

Also I showed a little package of tracts in rhyme I was distributing to the best people: *The Wings of the Morning*, or *The Tree of Laughing Bells.*[1] I hinted he might become

[1] This appears, pages seventy-four through eighty-one, in *General Booth and Other Poems.*

the possessor of one. I drew his attention
to the fact that there was no purse in the
exhibit. I divided my last four ginger-snaps
with him. I showed him a letter commending
me to all pious souls from a leading religious
worker in New York, Charles F. Powlison.

Soon we were thundering away to Valdosta!
Mr. Temperance climbed to the observation
chair in the little box at the top of the caboose,
alternately puzzling over my *Wings of the
Morning*,[1] and looking out. The caboose
bumped like a farm-wagon on a frozen road.
The pine-burning stove roared. The negro
Adonis on the wood-pile had gold in his teeth.
He had eyes like dark jewels set in white
marble, and he polished lanterns as black as
himself.

"By Jove," I said. "That's the handsomest
bit of lacquer this side of the Metropolitan
Museum."

"'Sh," said Conductor Roundface, sobering
himself. "You will queer yourself with the
old man. He wouldn't let that drummer on
because *he* swore."

---

[1] This appears, pages seventy-four through eighty-one, in
General Booth and Other Poems.

The old man came down. I bridled my profane tongue while he lectured the conductor on the necessity for more interest in the Georgia public schools, and the beauty of total abstinence, and, at last, the Japanese situation. This is a condensed translation of his speech: "I was on the side of the Russians all through the Russo-Japanese war. My friends said, 'Hooray for Japan.' But I say a Japanese is a nigger. I have never seen one, but I have seen their pictures. The Lord intended people to stay where they were put. We ought to have trade, but no immigration. Chinese belong to China. They are adapted to the Chinese climate. Niggers belong to Africa. They are adapted to the African climate. Americans belong to America. They are adapted to the American climate. Why, the mixing that is going on is something scandalous. I had a nigger working for me once that was half-Spaniard and half-Indian. There are just a few white people, and more mulattoes every day. The white people ought to keep their blood pure. Russians are white people. Germans, English, and Americans are white people. French people are niggers. Dagoes are niggers.

Jews are niggers. All people are niggers but just these four. There is going to be a big war in two or three years between all the white people and all the niggers. The niggers are going to combine and force a fight, Japan in the lead."

We reached Valdosta after dark. Conductor and inspector exchanged with me most civil good-bys. Their hospitality had been nepenthe for my poor broken heart. I reconciled myself to sitting in front of the station fireplace all night. I thought my nearest friend was at Macon, one hundred and fifty miles north; a gay cavalier who had read Omar Khayyam with me in college.

Just then an immense, angular, red-haired man sat down in front of the fire. He might have been the prodigal son of some Yankee farmer-statesman. He threw his arms around me, and though I had never seen him before, the Brotherhood of Man was established at once. He cast an empty bottle into the wood-box. He produced another. I would not drink. He poured down one-half of it. It snorted like dish-water going into the sink. He said: "That's right. Don't drink. This is the first time I ever drank. I have been on a soak two weeks. You see I was in Texas a long time, and went broke. I don't know how I got here." "Well," I said, "we have this fire till they run us out. Enjoy yourself."

He wept. "I don't deserve to enjoy anything. Anybody that's made a fool of himself as I have done. I wish I were in Vermont where my wife and babies are buried. Somebody wrote me they were dead and buried just when I went broke."

Thereafter he was merry. "There was a man in Vermont I didn't like who kept a fire like this. I went to see him every evening because I liked his fire. He would study and I would smoke."

He took out two dimes. "Say, that's my last money. Let's buy two tickets to the next station and get off and shoot up the town."

A hollow-eyed little man of middle age, grimy like a coal-miner, sat down on the other side of Mr. Vermont. He said he had been flagging trains for so long he could not tell when he began. He said he must wait three hours for a friend. He declined the bottle. He listened to Mr. Vermont's story,

told with variations. He put his chin into
his hands, his elbows on his knees, and slept.
Vermont threw himself on top of the bent
back, his face wrapped in his arms, like a
school-boy asleep on his desk-lid. Mr. Flagman slowly awoke, and cast off his brother,
and slept again. Cautiously Vermont waited,
to resume his pillow in a quarter of an hour,
and be again cast off.

Mr. Flagman sat up. I asked him if there
was a train for Macon going soon. He said:
"The through freight is making up now."
He gave me the conductor's name. I asked
if there was any one about who could write
me a pass to Macon. He said, "The pay car
has just come in, and Mr. Grady can give
you a pass if he wants to." I went out to the
tracks.

From a little window at the end of the car
Mr. Grady was paying the interminable sons
of Ham, who emerged from the African night,
climbed the steps, received their envelopes,
and slunk down the steps into the African night.

At last I showed Mr. Grady my letter from
Charles F. Powlison. Mr. Grady did not ap-
pear to be of a religious turn. I asked him

permission to ride to Macon in the caboose of the freight, going out at one o'clock. I assured him it was beneath my dignity to crawl into the box-car, or patronize the blind baggage, and I was tired of walking in swamp. Mr. Grady asked, "Are you an official of the road?"

"No, sir."

"Then what you ask is impossible, sir."

"Oh, my dear Mr. Grady, it is not impossible —"

"I am glad to have met you, sir. Goodnight, sir," and Mr. Grady had shut the window.

There was the smash, clang, and thud of making up a train. A negro guided me to the lantern of a freight conductor. The conductor had the lean frame, the tight jaw, the fox nose, the Chinese skin of a card-shark. He would have made a name for himself on the Spanish Main, some centuries since, by the cool way he would have snatched jewels from ladies' ears and smiled when they bled. He did not smile now. He gripped his lantern like a cutlass, and the cars groaned. They were gentlemen in armor compelled to walk the plank by this pirate with the apple-green eyes. We will call him Mr. Shark.

I put my pious letter into my pocket. "Mr. Shark, I would like to ride to Macon in the caboose." Mr. Shark thrust his lantern under my hat-brim. I had no collar, but was not ashamed of that. He said, "I have met men like you before." He turned down the track shouting orders. I jumped in front of him. I said, "You are mistaken. You have not met a man like me before. I am the goods. I am the wise boy from New York. I have been walking in every swamp in Florida, eating dead pig for breakfast, water-moccasins for lunch, alligators for dinner. I would like to tell you my adventures."

Mr. Shark ignored me, and went on persecuting the train.

Valdosta was a depot in the midst of darkness. I hated the darkness. I went into the depot. Vermont was offering Flagman the bottle. He drank.

Flagman asked me: "Can't you make it?"

"No. Grady turned me down. And the conductor turned me down."

Mr. Flagman said, "The sure way to ride

in a caboose like a gentleman is to ask the conductor like he is a gentleman, and everybody else is a gentleman, and when he turns you down, ask him again like a gentleman." And much more with that refrain. It was wisdom lightly given, profounder than it seemed. Let us remember the tired flagman, and engrave the substance of his saying on our souls.

I sought the pirate again. I took off my hat. I bowed like Don Cæsar De Bazan, but gravely. "I ask you, just as one gentleman to another, to take me to Macon. I have friends in Macon."

Mr. Shark showed a pale streak of smile. "Come around at one o'clock."

My "Thank you" was drowned by a late passenger. It came from Fargo, for Napoleon III dismounted. He said: "Hello. Where are you going, boy?"

"I am just taking the caboose of the through freight for Macon. But I have a few minutes."

"How the devil did you get here, sir?" I told him the story in brief. We were in front of the fire now. "How are you going to make this next train? I would like to go with you."

I could not tell whether he meant it or not.
Right beside us Mr. Flagman was asleep for
all night, with his elbows on his knees, his
chin in his hands. Stretched above Flagman's
back was Mr. Vermont, like a school-boy
asleep on his desk. I said, "Do you see the
gentleman on the bottom of the pile? He is
the Grand Lama of Cabooseville. You have
to ask him for the password. The man on
top is the sublime sub-Lama."

Napoleon looked dubiously at them, and the
two bottles in the wood-box. He gave me
good words of farewell, finishing with mock-
gravity : "Of course I respect you, sir, in not
giving the password without orders from your
superior, sir."

And now I boarded the caboose, hurrying
to surprise the Macon cavalier. He expected
me in three weeks, walking. But the caboose
did one hundred and fifty miles in thirteen
hours, and all the way my heart spun like a
glorified musical top. Alas, this is a tale of
drink. I filled the coffee-pot and drained it
an infinite number of times, all because my
poor broken heart was healed. The stove was
the only person in the world out of humor.

He was mad because his feet were nailed to the floor. He tried to spill the coffee, and screamed, "Now you've done it" every time we rounded a curve. The caboose-door slammed open every seven minutes, Shark and his white man and his negro rushing in from their all-night work for refreshment.

The manner of serving coffee in a caboose is this: there are three tin cups for the white men. The negro can chew sugar-cane, or steal a drink when we do not look. There is a tin box of sugar. If one is serving Mr. Shark, one shakes a great deal of sugar into the cup, and more down one's sleeve, and into one's shoes and about the rocking floor. One becomes sprinkled like a doughnut, newly-fried, and fragrant with splashed coffee. The cinders that come in on the breath of the shrieking night cling to the person. But if you are serving Mr. Shark you do not mind these things. You pour his drink, you eat his bread and cheese, thanking him from the bottom of your stomach, not having eaten anything since the ginger-snaps of long ago. You solemnly touch your cup to his, as you sit with him on the red disembowelled car cushions, with the moss gushing out. You wish him the treasure-heaps of Aladdin or a racing stable in Ireland, whichever he pleases.

Let all the readers of this tale who hope to become Gentlemen of the Road take off collars and cuffs, throw their purses into the ditch, break their china, and drink their coffee from tinware to the health of Mr. Shark, our friend with the apple-green eyes. Yea, my wanderers, the cure for the broken heart is gratitude to the gentleman you would hate, if you had your collar on or your purse in your pocket when you met him. Though there was heavy betting against him, he becomes the Hero in a whirlwind finish. Patriarch and Flagman disputing for second, decision for Flagman.

THE WOULD–BE MERMAN

Mobs are like the Gulf Stream,
Like the vast Atlantic.
In your fragile boats you ride,
Conceited folk at ease.
Far beneath are dancers,
Mermen wild and frantic,
Circling round the giant glowing
Sea-anemones.

"Crude, ill-smelling voters, —
Herds," to you in seeming.
But to me their draggled clothes
Are scales of gold and red.
Ah, the pink sea-horses,
Green sea-dragons gleaming,
And knights that chase the dragons
And spear them till they're dead!

Wisdom waits the diver
In the social ocean —

D   33

Rainbow shells of wonder,
Piled into a throne.
I would go exploring
Through the wide commotion,
Building under some deep cliff
A pearl-throne all my own.

Yesterday I dived there,
Grinned at all the roaring,
Clinging to the corals for a flash,
Defying death.
Mermen came rejoicing,
In procession pouring,
Yet I lost my feeble grip
And came above for breath.

I would be a merman.
Not in desperation
A momentary diver
Blue for lack of air.
But with gills deep-breathing
Swim amid the nation —
Finny feet and hands forsooth,
Sea-laurels in my hair.

MACON

THE languid town of Macon, Georgia, will ever remain in my mind as my first island of respite after vagrancy. My friend C. D. Russell lent me his clothes, took me to his eating-place, introduced his circle. We settled the destiny of the universe several different ways in peripatetic discourse.

After one has ventured one hundred and fifty miles through everglades and spent twenty-four sleepless hours riding in freight-cabooses the marrow of his bones is marsh, his hair and clothes are moss, cinders and bark, his immortal soul is engine-smoke Feeling just so, I had entered Russell's law office. He was at court. I sent word by his partner that I had gone to school with him in Ohio, that I had mailed a postal last Sunday from Florida telling him I would arrive afoot in three weeks, — but here I was, already. The word was carried with Southern precision.

"There is a person in the office who went to school with you in Indiana."

"I did not go to school in Indiana."

"He has been walking in Mississippi and Alabama. He wrote you a postal six weeks ago."

"How does he look?"

"Like the devil. He is principally pants and shirt."

The cavalier knew who that was. He found me, took me to his castle, introduced civilization. CIVILIZATION is whiter than the clouds, and full of clear water. One enters it with a plunge. CULTURE is a fuzzy fabric with which one rubs in CIVILIZATION. After I had been intimate with these, I was admitted to SOCIETY: a suit of the cavalier's clothes. I looked like him then, all but head and hands. I regarded myself with awe, as a gorilla would if he found himself fading into a Gibson picture.

A chair is a sturdy creature. I wonder who captured the first one? Who put out its eyes and taught it to stand still? A table-cloth is ritualistic. How nobly the napkin defends the vest, while those glistening birds, the knife, the fork, the spoon, bring one food.

How did these things to eat get here among these hundreds of houses? One would think that if anything to eat were brought among so many men, there would be enough hungry ones to kill each other and spoil it with blood.

Why do people stop eating when they have had just a bit? Why not go on forever?

We were in another room. The cavalier showed on the table what he called his Bible: the letters of Lord Chesterfield. To one who has not slept in all his life, who has lived a thousand years on freight trains, books do not count much. But how ingenious is a white iron bed, how subtle are pillows, how over-whelming is sleep!

THE FALLS OF TALLULAH

(North Georgia)

I

THE CALL OF THE WATER

THE dust of many miles was upon me. I felt uncouth in the presence of the sun-dried stones. Here was a natural bathing-place. Who could resist it?

I climbed further down the cañon, holding to the bushes. The cliff along which the water rushed to the fall's foot was smooth and seemed artificially made, though it had been so hewn by the fury of the cataclysm in ages past.

I took off my clothes and put my shoulders against the granite, being obliged to lean back a little to conform to its angle. I was standing with my left shoulder almost touching the perilous main column of water. A little fall that hurried along by itself a bit nearer the bank flowed over me. It came with headway. Though it looked so innocent, I could scarcely hold up against its power.

But it gave me delight to maintain myself. The touch of the stone was balm to my walk-worn body and dust-fevered feet. Like a sacerdotal robe the water flowed over my shoulders and I thought myself priest of the solitude.

I stepped out into the air. With unwonted energy I was able to throw off the coldness of my wet frame. The water there at the fall's foot was like a thousand elves singing. "Joy to all creatures!" cried the birds. "Joy to all creatures! Glory, glory, glory to the wild falls!"

II

THE PIPING OF PAN

I was getting myself sunburned, stretched out on the warm dry rocks. Down over the steep edge, somewhere near the foot of the next descent I heard the pipes of Pan. Why should I dress and go?

I made my shoes and clothes into a bundle,

and threw them down the cliff and climbed over, clinging to the steep by mere twigs. I seemed to hear the piping as I approached the terrace at the fall's base. Then the sound of music blended with the stream's strange voice and I turned to merge myself again with its waters.

Against the leaning wall of the cliff I placed my shoulders. The descending current smote me, wrestling with wildwood laughter, threatening to crush me and hurl me to the base of the mountain. But just as before my feet were well set in a notch of the cliff that went across the stream, cut there a million years ago.

It was a curious combination to discover, this stream-wide notch, and above it this wall with the water spread like a crystal robe over it. In the centre of the fall a Cyclops could have stood to bathe, and on the edge was the same provision in miniature for feeble man. And it was the more curious to find this plan repeated in detail by successive cataracts of the cañon, unmistakably wrought by the slow hand of geologic ages. And to see the water of the deep central stream undisturbed in the midst of the fall and still crystalline, and to see it slide down the steep incline and strike each notch at the foot with sudden music and appalling foam, was more wonderful than the simple telling can explain.

Each sheet of crystal that came over my shoulders seemed now to pour into them rather than over them. I lifted my mouth and drank as a desert bird drinks rain. My downstretched arms and extended fingers and the spreading spray seemed one. My heart with its exultant blood seemed but the curve of a cataract over the cliff of my soul.

III

PERIL, VANITY, AND ADORATION

Led by the pipes of Pan, I again descended. Once more that sound, almost overtaken, interwove itself with the water's cry, and I merged body and soul with the stream and the music. The margin of another cataract crashed upon me. In the recklessness of pleasure, one arm swung into the main current. Then the water threatened my life. To save myself, I was kneeling on one knee. I reached out blindly and found a hold at last in a slippery cleft, and later, it seemed an age, with the other hand I was able to reach one leaf. The leaf did not break. At last its bough was in my grasp and I crawled frightened into the sun. I sat long on a warm patch of grass.

But the cliffs and the water were not really my enemies. They sent a wind to give me delight. Never was the taste of the air so sweet as then. The touch of it was on my lips like fruit. There was a flattery in the tree-limbs bending near my shoulders. They said, "There is brotherhood in your footfall on our roots and the touch of your hand on our boughs."

The spray of the splashed foam was wine. I was the unchallenged possessor of all of nature my body and soul could lay hold upon. It was the fair season between spring and summer when no one came to this place. Like Selkirk, I was monarch of all I surveyed. In my folly I seemed to feel strange powers creeping into my veins from the sod. I forgot my near-disaster. I said in my heart, "O Mother Earth majestical, the touch of your creatures has comforted me, and I feel the strength of the soil creeping up into my dust. From this patch of soft grass, power and courage come up into me from your bosom, from the foundation of your continents. I feel within me the soul of iron from your iron mines, and the soul of lava from your deepest fires."

IV

THE BLOOD UNQUENCHABLE

The satyrs in the bushes were laughing at me and daring me to try the water again.

I stood on the edge of the rapids where were many stones coming up out of the foam. I threw logs across. The rocks held them in place. I lay down between the logs in the liquid ice. I defied it heartily. And my brother the river had mercy upon me, and slew me not.

Amid the shout of the stream the birds were singing: "Joy, joy, joy to all creatures, and happiness to the whole earth. Glory, glory, glory to the wild falls."

I struggled out from between the logs and threw my bundle over the cliff, and again descended, for I heard the pipes of Pan, just below me there, too plainly for delay. They seemed to say "Look! Here is a more exquisite place."

The sun beat down upon me. I felt myself twin brother to the sun. My body was lit with an all-conquering fever. I had walked through tropical wildernesses for many a mile, gathering sunshine. And now in an afternoon I was gambling my golden heat against the icy silver of the river and winning my wager, while all the leaves were laughing on all the trees.

And again I stood in a Heaven-prepared place, and the water poured in glory upon my shoulders.

*   *   *   *   *   *   *

Why was it so dark? Was a storm coming? I was dazed as a child in the theatre beholding the crowd go out after the sudden end of a solemn play. My clothes, it appeared, were half on. I was kneeling, looking up. I counted the falls to the top of the cañon. It was night, and I had wrestled with them all. My spirit was beyond all reason happy. This was a day for which I had not planned. I felt like one crowned. My blood was glowing like the blood of the crocus, the blood of the tiger-lily.

And so I meditated, and then at last the chill of weariness began to touch me and in my heart I said, "Oh Mother Earth, for all my vanity, I know I am but a perishable flower in a cleft of the rock. I give thanks to you who have fed me the wild milk of this river, who have upheld me like a child of the gods throughout this day."

Around a curve in the cañon, down stream, growing each moment sweeter, I heard the pipes of Pan.

V

The Gift of Tallulah

Go, you my brothers, whose hearts are in sore need of delight, and bathe in the falls of Tallulah. That experience will be for the foot-sore a balm, for the languid a lash, for the dry-throated pedant the very cup of nature. To those crushed by the inventions of cities, wounded by evil men, it will be a washing away of tears and of blood. Yea, it will be to them all, what it was to my heart that day, the sweet, sweet blowing of the reckless pipes of Pan.

THE GNOME

LET us now recall a certain adventure among the moonshiners.

When I walked north from Atlanta Easter morning, on Peachtree road, orchards were flowering everywhere. Resurrection songs flew across the road from humble blunt steeples.

Stony Mountain, miles to the east, Kenesaw on the western edge of things, and all the rest of the rolling land made the beginning of a gradual ascent by which I was to climb the Blue Ridge. The road mounted the watershed between the Atlantic and the gulf.

An old man took me into his wagon for a mile. I asked what sort of people I would meet on the Blue Ridge. He answered, "They make blockade whisky up there. But if you don't go around hunting stills by the creeks, or in the woods away from the road, they'll be awful glad to see you. They are all moonshiners, but if they likes a man they loves him, and they're as likely to get to lovin' you as not."

When I was truly in the mountains, six days north of Atlanta, a day's journey from the last struggling railway, the road wound into a certain high, uninhabited valley. Two days back, at a village I entered just after I had enjoyed the falls of Tallulah, I had found a letter from my new friend John Collier whom I had met in Macon and Atlanta. It contained a little money, which he insisted I should take, to make easier my way. I was inconsistent enough to spend some of it, instead of returning it or giving it "to the poor."

I invested seventy-five cents in brogans made of the thickest leather. I had thought they were conquered the first day. But now one of them bit a piece out of my heel. John Collier has done noble things since. On my behalf, for instance, he climbed Mount Mitchell with me, and showed me half the glory of the South. Then and after, he has helped my soul with counsel and teaching. But he should not have corrupted a near-Franciscan with money for hoodoo brogans. Though it was fairly warm weather, if ever I rested five minutes, the heavy things stiffened like cooling metal.

The little streams I crossed scarcely afforded me a drink.   Their dried borders had the footprints of swine on them.

Lameness affects one's vision.   The thick woods were the dregs of the landscape, fit haunt for the acorn-grubbing sow.   The road following the ridges was a monster's spine.

Those wicked brogans led me where they should not.   Or maybe it was just my destiny to find what I found.

About four o'clock in the afternoon, after exploring many roads that led to futile nothing, I was on what seemed the main highway, and dragged myself into the sight of the first mortal since daybreak.   He seemed like a gnome as he watched me across the furrows.   And so he was, despite his red-ripe cheeks.   The virginal mountain apple-tree, blossoming overhead, half covering the toad-like cabin, was out of place.   It should have been some fabulous, man-devouring devil-bush from the tropics, some monstrous work of the enemies of God.

The child, just in her teens, helping the Gnome to plant sweet potatoes, had in her life planted many, and eaten few. Or so it appeared. She was a crouching lump of earth. Her father dug the furrow. She did the planting, shovelling the dirt with her hands. Her face was sodden as any in the slums of Chicago. She ran to the house a ragged girl, and came back a homespun girl, a quick change. It must not be counted against her that she did not wash her face.

The Gnome talked to me meanwhile. He had made up his mind about me. "I guess you want to stay all night?"

"Yes."

"The next house is fifteen miles away. You are welcome if what we have is good enough for you. My wife is sick, but she will not let you be any bother."

I wanted to be noble and walk on. But I persuaded myself my feet were as sick as the woman. I accepted the Gnome's invitation.

Let the readers with a detective instinct note that his hoe-handle was two feet short, and had been whittled a little around the top to make it usable. It was at best an awkward instrument. (The mystery will soon be solved.)

We were met at the door by one my host

E

called Brother Joseph — a towering shape with an upper lip like a walrus, for it was armed with tusk-like mustaches. He was silent as King Log.

But the Gnome said, "I have saved up a month of talk since the last stranger came through." With ease, with simplicity of word, with I know not how much of guile, he gave fragments of his life: how he had lived in this log house always, how his first wife died, how her children were raised by this second wife and married off, how they now enjoyed this second family.

He showed me the other fragment of the hoe-handle. "I broke that over a horse's head the last time I was drunk. I always get crazy. When I come to, I do not remember anything about it. The last time I fought with my cousin. When I knocked down his horse he drew his knife. I drew *this* knife. My wife said I fought like a wild hog. I sliced my cousin pretty bad. He skipped the country, for he cut out one of my lungs and two of my ribs. I lost two buckets of blood. It took the doctor a long time to put my insides back."

From this hour forward he struggled between the luxury of being even more confidential, and the luxury of being cautious like a lynx. I squirmed. Despite his abandon, he was watching me.

I put one hand in my pocket. I found a diversion, a pair of eyeglasses. I had chanced on them in the bushes at Tallulah. The droop of his eyelids as he put them on was exquisite. He paced the floor. I had a review of his appearance. He was like a thin twist of tobacco. He had been burned out by too-sharp whisky. The babies clapped their hands as he strutted. He was like a third-rate Sunday-school teacher in a frock coat in the presence of the infant class. He was glad to keep the glasses, yet asked questions with a double meaning, implying I had stolen them in Atlanta, and fled these one hundred miles. We were gay rogues, and we knew it.

"Get up! Make some coffee and supper!" he shouted to the figure on the bed in the black corner of the cabin. He kept his jaw tight on his pipe, speaking to her in the gnome language. She replied in kind, snorting and muffling her words, without moving lips or

tongue, and keeping her teeth on her snuff-
stick. She stumbled up, groaning, with both
hands on her head. She had once been a
woman. She had lived with this thing too
long. All the trappings that make for home
had grown stale and weird about her. The
scraps of rag-carpet on the floor were rat
eaten. The red calico window curtains were
vilely dirty from the years of dust and the
leak of many rains. The benches were battered, unsteady. The door-latch was gone.
The door was held in place by a stone. She
stood before me, her hair hanging straight across
her face or down her collar, or flying about
or tied behind in a dreadful knot. She stood
before me, but as long as I was in that house
she did not look at me, she did not speak to me.

There was no stove. The Gnome said:
"Wife don't like a stove. She had rather
cook the way she learned." We rolled in the
back-log for her and coaxed up the embers.
We sat at one side of the hearth. We exchanged boastful adventures. She crawled into
the fireplace to nurse the corn-bread and coffee
and pork to perfection and place the Dutch
oven right.

Have you heard your grandmother speak of the Dutch oven? It is a squat kettle which is set in the embers. When it is hot, the biscuit dough is put in and the lid replaced. Slowly the biscuits become ambrosia. Slowly the watching cook is baked.

The Devil was in my host. By his coaxing hospitality he made it seem natural that a woman deadly sick should serve us. The rest of the family could wait. It did not matter if the tiny one cried and pulled the mother's skirt. She smote it into silence and fear, then carried it to the black corner where the potato planter herded the rest of the babies, helped by King Log, the walrus-headed.

The Gnome said, "I quit drinking ever since I had that fight I told you about. I don't dare drink. So I take coffee."

You should have seen him flooding himself with black coffee, drinking from a yellow bowl. I said to myself: "He will surely turn to the consolation of liquor anon. He will beat his wife again. He will drive his children into the woods. This woman must fight the battle for her offspring till her black-snake hair is white. Or maybe that insane knife will go

suddenly into her throat. She may die soon
with her hair black, — and red."

We ate with manly leisure. We were sated.
The mother prepared the second meal, and
called the group from the black corner. She
made ready her own supper. I see her by
the fire, the heavy arm shielding her face, the
hunched figure a knot of roots, — a palpable
mystery about her, making her worthy of a
portrait by some new Rembrandt. It is the
tragic mystery born of the isolation of the
Blue Ridge and the juice of the Indian corn.
Let us not forget the weapon with which she
fights the flame, the quaint long shovel.

Let us watch her at the table, breaking her
corn-bread alone, her puffy eyelids closed,
her cheek-bones seeming to cut through the
skin. There is something of the eagle in her
aspect because of her Roman nose, and her
hands moving like talons. It is not corn-bread
that she tears and devours. She is consuming
her enemies, which are Weariness, Squalor,
Flat and Unprofitable Memory, Spiritual Death.
She is seeking to forget that the light of the
hearthstone that falls on her dirty but beautiful babies is kindled in hell.

The Gnome spoke of his hogs. A Middle West farmer can talk hogs, and the world will admire him the more. But a mediæval swineherd dare not. It is self-betrayal.

My host grew affectionate, grandfatherly. He told of a solid acre of mica on top of a mountain. He speculated that it was a mile deep. He put a chunk into my pocket for me to carry to Asheville to interest great capitalists. He offered me fifty per cent on the profits. I took out a copy of the *Tree of Laughing Bells* from my pocket. I reviewed the tale contained in the book, in words I thought the Gnome would understand. Then he read it for himself with the "specs." He was proud of having learned to read out of the Bible, with no schooling.

He seemed particularly impressed with the length of the journey of the hero of the poem, who flew "to the farthest star of all." He looked at me with conceited shrewdness. "I played hookey myself, when I was a kid. I rode and walked forty-five miles that day. I was mighty glad to get back to my mammy the day after. I never wanted to run away again." He shook his pipe at me. "You are just a run-away boy, that's what you are."

He said something favorable about me to his wife, in the gnome language. She stood up. She shrilled back a caution. She showed her dirty teeth at him. But there was something he was bursting to tell me. He was essentially too reckless to conceal a secret long, even a life-and-death secret. He began: "I still raise a little corn."

The Walrus gave a sort of watch-dog bark. The Gnome reluctantly accepted the caution. He pointed sharply to the bed farthest from the black corner of the room.

"That's for you."

"Isn't there a shed or a corn-crib where I can sleep?"

"No, you don't get out of this house to-night. There aren't any sheds or cribs."

I looked helplessly around that single-roomed cabin. Not fear, but modesty, overcame me. I was expected to retire first. But King Log, the Walrus, perceiving my diffidence, set me an example. He rapidly hauled a couch off the porch and tumbled into it, first undressing as far as his underwear. With a quilt almost to his chin, and covering his pretty pink feet, he was a decent spectacle.

Happily I also wore underwear, and was soon under my quilt. I stole a look at the potato planter. I realized that she was the maiden present. Be pleased, O brothers, to observe that she has been aware of her age and state. She has huddled up to the fire, with her back to us; she has hidden her face on her knees. At last she piles ashes on the embers and finds a place in the black corner in the cot full of children. Her father and mother take the cot between.

Next morning was Sunday, a week since Easter. Only when a man has sadly mangled feet, and blood heated by many weeks of adventure, can he find luxury such as I found in the icy stream next morning. The divine rivulet on the far side of the field had been misnamed "Mud Creek." It was clear as a diamond.

Always carrying a piece of soap in my hip pocket, I was able to take a complete scour. Not content with this (pardon me), I did scrub shirt, socks, underwear, and bandanna. I hung them on the bushes, thanking God for the wind. Taking my before-mentioned credentials from my pocket, I made myself into a gentleman. When I dressed at last, my clothes were a little damp, but I knew that an hour's walking would put all to rights. As I held the bushes aside I saw a crib-like structure that made me shake more than the damp clothes. Was it a still, or was it not a still?

In my innocence I could not tell. But I remembered the warning, "Don't go pokin' round huntin' stills by the creeks."

As I hurried to the house my host carelessly appeared from the region of my bathing-place. He was whittling with his historic knife. I suppose he had noted my actions enough to restore his confidence. Anyway, the shame of being unwashed was his only visible emotion. He said, "I always bathe in hot water."

"So do I, when I am not on the road."

Still he was abashed. He took an enormous chew of tobacco to vindicate himself.

After breakfast the wife helped the Walrus to drag the cot out of doors. When she was alone on the porch I told her how sorry I was she had been obliged to cook for me. I thanked her for her toil. But she hurried away, without a pause or a glance. She kissed one of those

miry faced babies. She walked into the house,
leaving me smirking at the hills. She growled
something at the host. He came forth. He
pointed out the road, over the mountains and
far away. He broke off a blossoming apple-
sprig and whittled it.

"So you've been to Atlanta?" he asked.

"Yes."

"I was there once. What hotel did you use?"

"The Salvation Army."

"I was in the United States Hotel."

Still I was stupid. He continued:

"I was there two years."

He put on his glasses. He threw down the
apple-sprig, and, looking over the glasses, he
made unhappy each blossom in his own peculiar
way. He continued: "I was in the United
States Hotel, for making blockade whisky. I
don't make it any more." He spat again.
"I don't even go fishin' on Sunday unless —"

He had made up his mind that I was a customer, not a detective.

"Unless what?"

"Unless a visitor wants a mess of fish."

But I did not want a mess of fish. Re-
peatedly I offered money for my night's lodging.

This he declined with real pride. *He maintained his one virtue intact.* And so I thought of him, just as I left, as a man who kept his code.

The John Collier brogans were easier that morning, partly because I had something new on my mind, no doubt.

I thought of the Gnome a long time. I thought of the wife, and wondered at her as a unique illustration of the tragic mysteries of the human race. If she screams when seven devils enter into the Gnome, no one outside the house will hear but the apple-tree. If she weeps, only the wind in the chimney will understand. If she seeks justice and the law, King Log, the Walrus, is her uncertain refuge. If she desires mercy, the emperor of that valley, the king above King Log, is a venomous serpent, even the Worm of the Still.

But now the road unwound in glory. I walked away from those serpent-bitten dominions for that time. I was one with the air of the sweet heavens, the light of the ever-enduring sun, the abounding stillness of the forest, and the inscrutable Majesty, brooding on the mountains, the Majesty whom ignorantly we worship.

THE TRAMP'S REFUSAL

On Being Asked by a Beautiful Gipsy to Join her Group
of Strolling Players.

LADY, I cannot act, though I admire
God's great chameleons, Booth-Barret men.
But when the trees are green, my thoughts may
      be
October-red.   December comes again
And snowy Christmas there within my breast
Though I be walking in the August dust.
Often my lone contrary sword is bright
When every other soldier's sword is rust.
Sometimes, while churchly friends go up to God
On wings of prayer to altars of delight
I walk and talk with Satan, call him friend,
And greet the imps with converse most polite.
When hunger nips me, then at once I knock
At the near farmer's door and ask for bread.
I must, when I have wrought a curious song
Pin down some stranger till the thing is read.
When weeds choke up within, then look to me
To show the world the manners of a weed.

I cannot change my cloak except my heart
Has changed and set the fashion for the deed.
When love betrays me I go forth to tell
The first kind gossip that too-patent fact.
I cannot pose at hunger, love or shame.
It plagues me not to say : "I cannot act."
I only mourn that this unharnessed *me*
Walks with the devil far too much each day.
I would be chained to angel-kings of fire.
And whipped and driven up the heavenly way.

THE HOUSE OF THE LOOM

A Story of Seven Aristocrats and a Soap-Kettle.

WITH no sorrow in my heart, with no money in my pocket, with no baggage but a lunch, the most dazzling feature of which was a piece of gingerbread, I walked away from a wind-swept North Carolina village, one afternoon, over the mountain ridges toward Lake Toxaway. I turned to the right once too often, and climbed Mount Whiteside. There was a drop of millions of miles, and a Lilliputian valley below like a landscape by Charlotte B. Coman. I heard some days later that once a man tied a dog to an umbrella and threw him over. Dog landed safely, barking still. Dog was able to eat, walk, and wag as before. But the fate of the master was horrible. Dog never spoke to him again.

Having no umbrella, I retraced my way. I stepped into the highway that circumscribes the tremendous amphitheatre of Cashier's Valley. I met not a soul till eight o'clock that night. The mountain laurel, the sardis bloom, the violet, and the apple blossom made glad the margins of the splendidly built road; and, as long as the gingerbread lasted, I looked upon these things in a sort of sophisticated wonder.

This was because the gingerbread was given me by a civilized man, to whom John Collier had written for me a letter of introduction: Mr. Thomas G. Harbison, Botanical Collector; American tree seeds a specialty.

Back there by the village he was improving the breed of mountain apples by running a nursery. He was improving the children with a school he taught without salary, and was using the most modern pedagogy. Something in his manner made me say, "You are like a doctor out of one of Ibsen's plays, only you are optimistic." Then we talked of Ibsen. He debated art versus science, he being a science-fanatic, I an art-fanatic. He concluded the argument with these words: "You are bound to be wrong. I am bound to be wrong. What is the use of either of us judging the other?" That is not the mountain way of ending a discussion.

For the purposes of the tale, as well as for his own merits, we must praise this civilized man who entertained me a day and a half so well. His mountain cottage was a permanent civilized camp. Without intruding on his privacy, we can show what that means. Cross a few states to the west with me.

Have you watched the camps of the up-to-date visitors, in the oldest parts of Colorado? They begin with tent, axe, blanket, bacon, and frying-pan, as miners do. In ten summers, though they climb as much as the miners, wear uglier boots, and rougher clothes, their tents are highly organized. They are convenient and free from clutter as the best New York flat. The axe has multiplied rustic benches, bridges, shelters. It has made a refrigerator in the stream. The frying-pan has changed into a camp-stove and a box of white granite dishes. The blanket flowers and Mariposa lilies that made the aspen groves celestial have been gathered in jardinières.

Meanwhile, in the big houses of the veteran miners of the villages are the axe, the blanket, and the frying-pan, though their lords have been through half a dozen fortunes since

F

pioneer days. Those houses have the single great advantage of a rich tradition. They seem to grow up out of the ground.

Musing these matters, I munched my gingerbread, walking past sweet waterfalls, groves of enormous cedars, many springs, and one deserted cabin. I was homesick for that great civilized camp, New York, and the sober-minded pursuit of knowledge there.

But civilization lost her battle at twilight, when I swallowed my last gingerbread crumb. Immediately I was in the land beyond the nowhere place, willing to sleep twelve hours by a waterfall, or let the fairies wake me before day. The road went deeper into savagery. I blundered on, rejoicing in the fever of weariness. In the piercing light of the young stars, the house that came at last before me seemed even more deeply rooted in the ground than the oaks around it. What new revelation lies here? Knock, knock, knock, O my soul, and may Heaven open a mystery that will give the traveller a contrite heart.

Let us tell a secret, even before we enter. If, with the proper magic in our minds, we were guests here, a year or a day, we might write the world's one unwritten epic. All day, in one of these tiny rooms, amid appointments that fill the spirit with the elation of simple things, we would write. At evening we would dream the next event by the fire. The epic would begin with the opening of the door.

There appeared a military figure, with a face like Henry Irving's in contour, like Whistler's in sharpness, fantasy, and pride.

"May I have a night's lodging? I have no money."

"Come in. . . . We never turn a man away."

We were inside. He asked: "What might be your name?" I gave it. He gave his. The circle by the fire did not turn their heads, but presumably I was introduced. One child ran into the kitchen. My host gave me her chair. All looked silently into the great soap-kettle in the midst of the snapping logs.

I have a high opinion of the fine people of the South, and gratefully remember the scattering of gentlefolk so good as to entertain me in their mansions. But in this cottage, with one glance at those fixed, flushed faces, I said: "This is the best blood I have met in this

United States." The five children were night-blooming flowers. There were hints of Doré in the shadow of the father, cast against the log walls of the cabin. He sat on the little stairway. He was a better Don Quixote than Doré ever drew.

I said, "Every middle-aged man I have met in Florida, Georgia, and North Carolina has been a soldier, and I suppose you were."

He looked at me long, as though the obligation of hospitality did not involve conversation. He spoke at last: "I fought, but I could not help it. It was for home, or against home. I fought for this cabin."

"It is a beautiful cabin."

He relented a bit. "We have kept it just so, ever since my great-grandfather came here with his pack-mule and made his own trail. I — I hated the war. We did not care anything about the cotton and niggers of the fire-eaters. The niggers never climbed this high."

I changed the subject. "This is the largest fireplace I have seen in the South. A man could stand up in it."

He stiffened again. "*This is not the South. This is the Blue Ridge.*"

An inner door opened. It was plain the woman who stood there was his wife. She had the austere mouth a wife's passion gives. She had the sweet white throat of her youth, that made even the candle-flame rejoice. She looked straight at me, with ink-black eyes. She was dumb, like some one struggling to awake.

"Everything is ready," she said at length to her husband.

He turned to me: "Your supper is now in the kitchen, 'if what we have is good enough.'" It was the usual formula for hospitality.

I turned to the wife. "My dear woman, I did not know that this was going on. It is not right for you to set a new supper at this hour. I had enough on the road."

"But you have walked a long way." Then she uttered the ancient proverb of the Blue Ridge. "'A stranger needs takin' care of.'"

In the kitchen there was a cook-stove. Otherwise there was nothing to remind one of the world this side of Beowulf. I felt myself in a stronghold of barbarian royalty.

"Do you do your own spinning and weaving?"

She lifted the candle, lighting a corner.
"Here are the cards and the wools." She
held it higher. "There is the spinning wheel."

"Where is the loom?"

"Up stairs, just by where you will sleep."

I knew that if there was a loom, it was a
magic one, for she was a witch of the better
sort, a fine, serious witch, and a princess withal.
Her ancestors wore their black hair that simple
way when their lords won them by fighting
dragons. She was prouder than the pyramids.
If the epic is ever written, let it tell how the
spinner of the wizard wools did stand to serve
the stranger, that being the custom of her
house. This was a primitive camp indeed.
There was no gingerbread. There was not one
thing to remind me of the last table at which
I had eaten. But every gesture said, "Good
prince, you are far from your court. Therefore, this, our royal trencher, is yours. May
you find your way to your own kingdom in
peace." But for a long time her lips were
still. She had the spareness of a fertile, toiling
mother. And, ah, the motherhood in her
voice when she said at last, "My son, you are
tired."

Let the epic tell that, when the stranger returned to the fireplace, a restless, expectant silence settled down upon the circle. There was portent in the hiss of the flames. When I spoke to the children they only stared at me as at a curious shadow. Their lips moved not. The eldest, about seventeen, had inherited, no doubt, his love of strange brewing. He looked sideways into the soap-kettle. I said to myself, "He sees more hippogriffs than steam-engines." He eyed every move of the circle with restless approval or disapproval. Every chip his little brother threw on the fire seemed to be a symbol of some precious thing sacrificed, every curl of steam seemed to have something to do with the destiny of the house.

He took out of his pocket a monthly magazine. It was the sort that costs ten cents a year. No doubt, had he gone to school to the admirable man who gave me gingerbread, he would have learned to read scientific and technical monthlies. But a magazine of any sort is a terribly intrusive thing at this juncture. The boy, and a sister just a little younger, read in a loud whisper to one another an advertisement they did not want me to hear. At their stage of culture it was impossible to read silently. The advertisement, if I remember, went about this way: —

"Free, free, free! A sewing machine! Send us a two-cent stamp, your name and address, mentioning the name of this magazine. We will tell you how to get an up-to-date sewing machine absolutely free. This offer is good for thirty days."

They wrote a most unscholarly letter, spelling it aloud. It required their total and united culture to produce it. When the girl returned to the fire, she was provoked by her pride into an astonishing flush. How it set off her temples, with their pattern of azure veins! With her lotus-leaf hands, the hands of Hathor, goddess of love, she cooled her cheeks again and again. There is something of breeding in the very color of blood. Come, brothers of the road, all who travel with me in fancy, will you not join the knighthood of the soap-kettle? Come, ladies in mansions, will you not be one with us? None of you could have gainsaid the maiden-in-chief of the assembly. She wore her homespun as Zenobia, princess of Palmyra, wore her splendors. With

her arms around her two gypsy younger sisters
she smiled at last into the soap-kettle. When
the epic is written, let it use words of marvelling, speaking of her hair, so pale, so electrical,
set in a thick, ingenious coronal.

All the little children stood up. "Uncle,"
they shouted. Hoofs sounded by the door.
A man entered without knocking. When he
saw me he became ceremonious as a Mandarin.

"This is a traveller," said my host.

The messenger indulged in inquiries about
my welfare, journey, and destination. My host
interrupted.

"How's mother? We have watched late to
know."

"She is much worse." And the messenger
went on to say that she might not live two
days, and the doctor was a careless, indifferent
dog, treating her as though she were an ordinary
old woman.

"Does he still give her strychnine?"

"He won't deny it." The messenger explained that the doctor thought strychnine in
small doses was good for old people. The
scientist who gave me gingerbread should have
been there to champion the doctor. In the

eyes of his judges that night he was suspected of poisoning or treating with criminal folly, royalty itself.

The younger doctor was miles away, and might refuse to make the trip. The two loyal sons seemed paralyzed because the time for decision and the time for mourning came together. There were long silences, interrupted by my host repeating in a sort of primitive song, "*I can't think of anything except my dying mother. I can't think of anything except mother is going to die.*"

At last, with his brother's consent, the messenger galloped and galloped away, to find his only hope, the younger physician. As the wife gave me the candle, sending me up stairs, I looked back at the family circle.

Helpless grief made every face rigid. I looked again at the eldest daughter. The moving shadows embroidered on her breast intricate symbols of the fair years, passing by in the ghost of tapestry, things that happened in the beginning of the world. Let the epic tell that when the stranger slept there was a magic loom by his bed that wove that history again in valiant colors, showing battles without

number, and sieges, and interminable sunny
love-tales, and lotus-handed ladies whispering
over manuscript things too fine to be told,
and ruddy warriors sitting at watch-fires on
battlements eternal; and let the epic tell
how, in the early dawn, the stranger half
awoke, yet saw this tapestry hung round the
walls. If one could remember every story for
which the pictures stood, he might indeed
write the world's unwritten epic. The last
tapestry to be hung changed from gold to
black warp and woof upon which was written
that because of a treacherous prime minister
who served a poisoned wine, the Empress of the
White Witches was perishing before her time,
and the young wizard, with the counter-spell,
was riding night and day, but all the palace
knew he would arrive too late.

At breakfast the faces were stolid and white
as frost. The father answered me only when
I said good-by.

He said he hardly knew whether I had had
anything to eat, or whether any one had been
good to me. "You just had to take care of
yourself." The son, feeling the demand of
hospitality in his father's voice, walked to the

road with me. He asked if I was walking to
Asheville.

"Yes, by way of Mount Toxaway and
Brevard."

He told me it was good walking all the way,
and added, in a difficult burst of confidence,
"I am going to Asheville."

"Why not come along with me?" I asked.
I meant it heartily.

He said he had to take horseback, and then
the railway. He had to be there to-morrow.

"What's the hurry?"

"I have to witness in a whisky case, an
internal revenue case."

He said it like a Spanish Protestant called
before the inquisition.

I said to my soul: "These were the revela-
tions of a night and a morning. What deeper
troubles were in the House of the Loom that
you did not know?"

All through the country there had been that
night what is called a black frost. By the
roadside it was deep and white as the wool on
a sheep. But it left things blighted and black,
and destroyed the chances of the fruit-bearing

trees. All the way to Mount Toxaway I met scattered mourners of the ill-timed visitation.

But the simple folly of spring was in me, and the strange elation of gratitude. My soul said within itself: "A money-claim has definite limits, but when will you ever discharge your obligation to the proud and the fine in the House of the Loom? You intruded on their grief. Yet they held their guest sacred as their grief."

PHIDIAS

Would that the joy of living came to-day,
Even as sculptured on Athena's shrine
In sunny conclave of serene design,
Maidens and men, procession flute and feast,
By Phidias, the ivory-hearted priest
Of beauty absolute, whose eyes the sun
Showed goodlier forms than our desires can
    guess
And more of happiness.

MAN, IN THE CITY OF COLLARS

A Not Very Tragic Relapse into the Toils of the World,
and of Finance.

HAVING been properly treated as a bunco
man by systematic piety in a certain city further
south, I had double-barrelled special recom-
mendations sent to a lofty benevolence in
Asheville, from a religious leader of New York,
the before-mentioned Charles F. Powlison.

It was with confidence that I bade good-by
to the chicken-merchant who drove me into
the city. I entered the office of the black-
coated, semi-clerical gentleman who had received the Powlison indorsements. My stick
pounded his floor. The heels of my brogans
made the place resound. But he gave all
official privileges. He received me with the
fine manly handclasp, the glitter of teeth, the
pat on the back. He insisted I use the shower
bath, writing room, reading table. Then I
suggested a conference among a dozen of his

devouter workers on the relation of the sense
of Beauty to their present notion of Christianity
or, if he preferred, a talk on some aspect of art
to a larger group.

He took me into his office.   He shut the door.
He was haughty.   He made me haughty.   I
give the conversation as it struck me.   He
probably said some smart things I do not
recall.   But I remember all the smart things
I said.

He denounced labor agitators in plain words.
I agreed.   I belonged to the brotherhood of
those who loaf and invite their souls.

He spoke of anarchy.   I maintained that I
loved the law.

He very clearly, and at length, assaulted
Single Tax.   I knew nothing then of Single
Tax, and thanked him for light.   He denounced
Socialism.   Knowing little about Socialism at
that time, I denounced it also, having just
been converted to individualism by a man in
Highlands.

The religious leader spoke of his long experience with bunco men.   I insisted I wanted not
a cent from him, I was there to do him good.
I had letters of introduction to two men in the

city; one of them, an active worker in the
organization, had already been in to identify
me. A third man was coming to climb Mount
Mitchell with me.

He doubted that I was a bona fide worker
in his organization. Then came my only long
speech. We will omit the speech. But he
began to see light. He took a fresh grip on
his argument. He said: "There is a man
here in Asheville I see snooping around with a
tin box and a butterfly net. They call him the
state something-ologist. He goes around and —
and — *hunts bugs*. But do you want to know
what I think of a crank like that?" I wanted
to know. He told me.

"But," I objected, "I am not a scientist. I
am an art student."

He expressed an interest in art. He gave
a pious and proper view of the nude in art. It
took some time. It was the sort of chilly,
cautious talk that could not possibly bring a
blush to the cheek of ignorance. I assured
him his decorous concessions were unnecessary.
I was not expounding the nude.

There was an artist here, and Asheville
needed no further instruction of the kind, he

G

maintained. The gentleman had won some blue ribbons in Europe. He painted a big picture (dimensions were given) and sold it for thousands (price was given).

"He is holding the next one, two feet longer each way, for double the money."

I told him if he felt there was enough art in Asheville, we might do something to popularize the poets.

In reply he talked about literary cranks. He spoke of how Thoreau, with his long hair and ugly looks, frightened strangers who suddenly met him in the woods. I thanked him for light on Thoreau. . . . But he had to admit that my hair was short.

He suspected I was neither artist nor literary man. I assured him my friends were often of the same opinion.

"But," he said bitterly, "do you know sir, by the tone of letters I received from Mr. Powlison I expected to assemble the wealth and fashion of Asheville to hear you. I expected to see you first in your private car, wearing a dress-suit."

I answered sternly, "Art, my friend, does not travel in a Pullman."

He threw off all restraint. "Old shoes," he said, "old shoes." He pointed at them.

"I have walked two hundred miles among the moonshiners. They wear brogans like these." But his manner plainly said that his organization did not need cranks climbing over the mountains to tell them things.

"Your New York letter did not say you were walking. It said you 'would arrive.'"

He began to point again. "Frayed trousers! And the lining of your coat in rags!"

"I took the lining of the coat for necessary patches."

"A blue bandanna round your neck!"

"To protect me from sunburn."

He rose and hit the table. "And no collar!"

"Oh yes, I have a collar." I drew it from my hip pocket. It had had a two hundred mile ride, and needed a bath.

"I should like to have it laundered, but I haven't the money."

"*Get* the money."

"No," I said, "but I will get a collar."

I entered a furnishing and tailor shop around the corner. I asked for the proprietor. He showed me collars.

"Two for a quarter?"

"Yes."

"Now I have here a little brochure I sell for twenty-five cents. In fact it is a poem, well worth the money. I will let you have it for half price, that is, one collar."

"We are selling collars."

"I am selling the poem."

I turned my Ancient Mariner eye on him. I recited the most mesmeric rhymes.

He repeated, "We are selling collars."

Evidently the eye was out of order. I tried argument.

"Don't you think I need a collar?"

"Yes."

"Don't you think this one would fit this shirt?"

"Yes."

"I renew my offer."

He sternly put the box away.

So I said, "If I must face my friends in Asheville without this necessary ornament, you shall blush. I have done my duty, and refuse to blush."

I looked up a scholar from Yale, Yutaka Minakuchi, friend of old friends, student of philosophy, in which he instructed me much, first lending me a collar. He became my host in Asheville. It needs no words of mine to enhance the fame of Japanese hospitality. . . .

And I had a friend in a distant place, whom, for fancy's sake, we will call the Caliph Haroun-al-Raschid. Let him remain a mystery. We will reveal this much. Had he known the truth, he would have sent Greek slaves riding on elephants, laden with changes of raiment. He discerned, at least, that I was in a barbarous land, for at length a long package containing a sword arrived from the court of the Caliph (to speak in parables). I exchanged the weapon at a pawnshop for *money*, all in one bill — *money* — against which I had so many times sworn eternal warfare, which had been my hoodoo in the past, and was destined to be again. But this time, such are the whims of fate, the little while it was with me it brought me only good.

I entered the furnishing store. The proprietor was terribly busy, but my glittering eye was in condition. I persuaded him, by dint of repetition, to show me his collars. I treated him as though we had not met.

"Fifteen cents apiece?"

"Yes."

"I will take *one*." I gave the bill. He had to send a boy out for the change. I put the silver in my pocket, and rattled it. He wrapped up the collar, while I studied his cheeks. He blushed like a maid, bless his tender heart, and in his sweet confusion he knew that I knew it.

The streets of Asheville kept shouting to me: "Let us praise Man, when he builds cities, and grows respectable, and cringes to money, and becomes a tailor, and loves collars with all his heart."

*   *   *   *   *   *   *

CONFUCIUS

WOULD we were scholars of Confucius' time
Watching the feudal China crumbling down,
Frightening our master, shaking many a crown,
Until he makes more firm the father sages,
Restoring custom from the earliest ages
With prudent sayings, golden as the sun.
Lord, show us safe, august, established ways,
Fill us with yesterdays.

THE OLD LADY AT THE TOP OF THE HILL

It was a bland afternoon. I had been crossing a green valley in North Carolina. Every man I passed had that languid leanness slanderously attributed to the hookworm by folk who have no temperament. Yet some bee of industry must have stung these fellows into intermittent effort this morning, yesterday, last week or last year.

Here were reasonably good barns. Here were fences, and good fences at that. Here were mysterious crops, neither cotton nor corn. One man was not ploughing with a mule. No, sir. He was ploughing with a sort of horse. . . .

At last I mounted the northern rim of the circle of steep hills that kept the place as separate from the rest of the world as a Chinese wall. I met her on the crest. She advanced slowly, looking on the ground, leaning at the hips as do the very aged, but not grotesquely. Her primly made dress and sunbonnet were dull dark blue. With her walking-stick she meditatively knocked the little stones from her path. The staff had a T-shaped head. It was the cane Old Mother Hubbard carries in the toy book.

And now she looked up and said with a pleasant start, "Why, good evening, young stranger."

"Good evening, kind lady."

"Where have you been, my son?"

"Why, I am following my nose to the end of the world. I have just walked through this enterprising valley."

She looked into the dust and meditated awhile. Then she said: "It's getting late. No one has let you in?"

"No one."

"How about that house by the bridge?" She pointed with her cane.

"The lady said she had a sick child."

"Nonsense, nonsense. Do you see that little Ardella by that corner of the ploughed field near the house? She don't run like a sick child. . . . Did you ask at the next place, the one that has a green porch?" She pointed again with her cane.

"The woman said she had no spare bed."

"But she has. I slept in it last week. . . .
And that last house before you start up this
hill?"

"The woman said she had to take care of
saw-mill hands."

"Did she tell you *that?*"

"Yes, ma'am."

The old lady ruminated again, leaning on
her stick. At length she said: "Sit down.
I want to tell you something." There we
were, Grandmother and newly adopted grand-
son, on a big sunlit rock.

I give only the spirit of her words. She
discoursed in that precious mountain dialect,
so mediæval, so Shakespearean with its sur-
prising phrases that seem at first the slang of
a literary clan, till one learns they are the
common property of folk that cannot read. It
is a manner of speech all too elusive. Would
that I had kept a note-book upon it! But
somewhat to this intent she spoke, and in a
tone gentler than her words: —

"They thought I would never find out about
this, or they would not have treated you so.
That woman in the last house is my daughter-

in-law. She has only two saw-mill hands, and they're no trouble. That's my house anyway. It was my mother's before me. No one dares turn strangers away when I am there. There's an empty bed up stairs, and another in the hall."

She turned about and pointed in the direction in which I had been walking. "Just ahead of you, around that clump of trees, is a hospitable family. If they will not take care of you, it is because they have a good excuse. If they cannot take you in, ask no further. Come back to my place, and" (she spoke with a Colonial Dame air) "*I will make you welcome.*"

"What sort of mountaineer is this?" I asked myself. "The hospitality is the usual thing, but the grandeur is exotic."

We chatted awhile of the sunset. Then I accompanied her to the edge of the hill.

Under her sacred hair her face retained girl-contours. The wrinkles were not too deep. She seemed not to have changed as mothers often do, when, under decades of inevitable sorrow, the features are recarved into the special mask of middle age, and finally into the very different mask of senility. She had yet the authority of Beauty. She wore her white hair with a Quakerish-feminine skill most admirably adapted to that ancient forehead. I divined she had learned that at sixteen. What a long time to be remembering.

We were spirits that at once met and understood. She said: "My son, I have walked all my life across this valley, or up this hill, or toward that green mountain where you are going. I never walked as far as I wanted to. But walking even so short a path makes for consolation."

Now she laid aside antique grandeur and took on plain vanity.

"Do you know how old I am?"

"About eighty-five."

"I'm ninety-two years old, young man, and I'm going to live ten years more."

It was getting late. I said, "I am glad indeed to have met you."

She answered, "I am sorry my valley has not been kind."

I ventured to ask, "So it's *your* valley?"

I had touched a raw nerve. I was completely shaken by the suddenness of her answer.

"Mine! Mine! Mine!" she shrieked. Kneeling, she beat up the dust of the road with her cane. And then "Mine! Mine! Mine!" shaking her outstretched arms over that amphitheatre, as though she would drag it all to her breast.

She was out of breath and trembling. At length she smiled, and added so quietly it seemed another person. "And they shall not take it away from me."

I helped her to her feet. She was once more the Martha Washington sort. . . . I remember her last sentence. In a royal tone, that was three times an accolade, in a motherly tone that was caressing and slow she half-sung the pretty words: —

"Good evening, young man. I wish you well."

The man at the next house took me in. In the course of the evening he assured me that the old lady did own the valley, and that she ruled it with a rod of iron. The family graveyard was full of heirs who had grown to old age and died of old age hoping in vain to outlive, and to inherit her authority.

WITH A ROSE, TO BRUNHILDE

BRUNHILDE, with the young Norn soul
That has no peace, and grim as those
That spun the thread of life, give heed:
Peace is concealed in every rose.
And in these petals peace I bring:
A jewel clearer than the dew:
A perfume subtler than the breath
Of Spring with which it circles you.

Peace I have found, asleep, awake,
By many paths, on many a strand.
Peace overspreads the sky with stars.
Peace is concealed within your hand.
And when at night I clasp it there
I wonder how you never know
The strength you shed from finger-tips:
The treasure that consoles me so.

Begin the art of finding peace,
Beloved: — it is art, no less.

Sometimes we find it hid beneath
The orchards in their springtime dress :
Sometimes one finds it in oak woods,
Sometimes in dazzling mountain-snows ;
In books, sometimes.   But pray begin
By finding it within a rose.

LADY IRON-HEELS[1]

I

THE SEVEN SUSPICIONS

ONE Saturday in May I was hurrying from mountainous North Carolina into mountainous Tennessee. Because of my speed and air of alarm, I was followed by the Seven Suspicions. I was either a revenue detective in pursuit of moonshiners, or a moonshiner pursued by revenue detectives, or a thief hurrying out of hot territory, or a deputy sheriff pursuing a thief, or a pretended non-combatant hurrying toward a Tennessee feud, actually an armed

---

[1] In the prose sketches in this book I have allowed myself a story-teller's license only a little. Sometimes a considerable happening is introduced that came the day before, or two days after. In some cases the events of a week are told in reverse order.

Lady Iron-Heels is obviously a story, but embodies my exact impression of that region in a more compressed form than a note-book record could have done.

The other travel-narratives are ninety-nine per cent literal fact and one per cent abbreviation.

recruit, or I had just killed my family's hereditary enemy and was eluding his avengers, or I
had bought some moonshine whisky and was
trying to get out of a bad region before night-
fall. These suspicions implied that the inhabitants admired me. Yet I hurried.

I came upon one article of my creed, the very
next day, Sunday. But Saturday was a season
of panic, preparation, and trial.

The article of my creed that I won as my re-
ward might be stated in this fashion: *"Peace
is to be found, even in a red and bleeding rose."*

I was accustomed to the feudist and the
assassin. Such people had been good to me,
and I had walked calmly through their haunts.
But now the smothering landscape seemed to
double every natural fear. The hills were so
steep and so close together that only the indomitable corn and rye climbed to the top
to see the sun. The road was in the bed of a
scolding rivulet. People in general travelled
horseback. Cross-logs for those afoot bridged
high above the streams every half mile. There
was a primeval something about the heavy
chains of the cross-logs, binding them to the
trees, that suggested the forgotten beginning

H

of an iron people, some harsh iron-willed Sparta. This impression was strengthened by the unpainted dwellings, hunched close to the path, with thick walls to resist siege.

What first fixed these outlaws here, as in a nest, with a ring of houseless open country round them? A traveller was more shut from the horizon than in the slums of Chicago. The road climbed no summits. It writhed like a snake. And there were snakes sunning themselves on every other cross-log. *And there was never a flower to be seen.*

An old woman, kindly enough, gave this beggar a noon-meal for the asking, but the landscape had struck into me so I almost feared to eat the bread. For this fear I sternly blamed my perverse imagination. Refreshed in body only, I crept like a fascinated fly, dragged by occult force toward a spider's den. I felt as though I had reached the very heart of the trap when I stepped into the streets of the profane village of Flagpond, Tennessee.

It was early in the afternoon. The feudal warriors had come to the place on horseback, dressed in poverty-stricken Saturday finery: clothes tight and ill-dyed, with black felt hats that should have slouched, but did not. The immaculate rims stood out in queer precision. The wearers sat in front of the three main stores, looking across the street at one another. Since there was no woman in sight, every one knew that the shooting might begin at any time. The silence was deadly as the silence of a plague. I checked my pace. I ambled in a leisurely way from store to store, inquiring the road to Cumberland Gap, the distance to Greenville, and the like. I was on the other side of the circle of dwellings pretty soon, followed by the Seven Suspicions, shot from about seventy-five lean countenances, which makes about five hundred and twenty-five suspicions.

One of the most indescribable and haunting things of that region was that all the women and children were dressed in a certain dead-bone gray.

About four o'clock I had made good my escape. I had begun to mount rolling, uninhabited hills. At twilight I entered a plain, and felt a new kind of civilization round me. It would have been shabby in Indiana. Here it was glorious. They had whitewashed fences, and white-painted cottages, glimmering kindly

through the dusk. Some farm machinery was
rusting in the open. I climbed a last year's
straw-stack, and slept, with acres of stars pouring down peace.

II

THE TAILOR AND THE FLORIST

Now the story begins all over again with
the episode of the well-known tailor and the
unknown florist. Just off the main street of
Greenville, Tennessee, there is a log cabin with
the century old inscription, ANDREW JOHNSON,
TAILOR. That sign is the fittest monument to
the indomitable but dubious man who could not
cut the mantle of the railsplitter to fit him. I
was told by the citizens of Greenville that there
was a monument to their hero on the hill. So
I climbed up. It was indeed wonderful — a
weird straddling archway, supporting an obelisk.
The archway also upheld two flaming funeral
urns with buzzard contours, and a stone eagle
preparing to screech. There was a dog-eared
scroll inscribed, "His faith in the people never
wavered." Around all was, most appropriately,
a spiked fence.

But I was glad I came, because near the Tailor's resting-place was a Florist's grave, on which depends the rest of this adventure, and which reaches back to the beginning of it. It had a wooden headstone, marked "John Kenton of Flagpond, Florist. 1870–1900." And in testimony to his occupation, a great rosebush almost hid the inscription. Any man who could undertake to sell flowers in Flagpond might have it said of him also, "His faith in the people never wavered."

And now in my tramping the spirit of John Kenton, or some other Florist, seemed to lead me. My season of panic, preparation, and trial was over. It was indeed Sunday on this planet for awhile. I passed bush after bush of the same sort as that marking Kenton's place of sleep. The sight of them was all that I had to give me strength till noon. I had had neither breakfast nor supper. People would have fed this poor tramp, but I love sometimes the ecstasy that comes with healthy fasting. And now that I reflect upon it, it was indeed appropriate that the Religion of the Rose should begin with abstinence.

I have burdened you further back with an

elaborate description of the landscape of Flagpond. Now that landscape was repeated with
the addition of roses. And what a difference they
made! They quenched the Seven Suspicions.
They made gray dresses seem rather tolerable.
On either side loomed the steepest cornfields
yet, but they did not make me tremble now.

At noon I turned aside where a log cabin on
stilts, leaning against its own chimney, stood
astride a little gully. It was about as big as a
dove-cote. Straggling rose-hedges led to the
green-banked spring at the foot of a ladder that
took the place of steps. The old lady that came
to the door was a dove in one respect only; she
was dressed in gray.

She was drawn to the pattern of the tub-like
peasants of the German funny paper *Simplicissimus*. I told her my name was Nicholas.
She took it for granted that I wanted my dinner,
and asked me up the ladder without ado. She
did an unusual thing. She began to talk family
affairs. "You must be kin to Lawyer Nicholas
of Flagpond. . . . He defended my son ten
years ago . . . in a trial for murder."

I said: "I am no kin to Lawyer Nicholas,
but I hope he won his case."

"No. My son is in the state's prison for life. . . . He surely killed Florist Kenton." But she added, as if it nullified all guilt, "they were both drunk."

She was busy cooking at the open fireplace. She turned to the boy, about ten years old. "Call your Ma and your Aunt to dinner." He climbed the steep and shouted. Presently two figures came over the ridge. The larger woman took the boy's hand.

"That's my daughter-in-law, the boy's mother," said Mrs. Simplicissimus.

I judged the second figure to be a woman of about twenty-eight. She carried a fence-rail on her shoulder. She was straight as an Indian. The old woman said: *"That's my daughter. She was going to marry John Kenton."* The only influences that could have induced a mountain-woman to unburden so much, were the roses, just outside the door, leaping in the wind.

The procession soon reached us. The wood-carrier threw the log into the yard. "There's firewood," she sang. She vaulted over the fence, displaying iron-heeled brogans, thick red stockings, and a red-lined skirt. There was a smear of earth on cheek and chin. Her face was a sunburned, dust-mired roseleaf. She swept off her hat. She bowed ironically. She said: "Howdy. What might be your name?"

I did not tell my name.

She fell on her knees. She drank from her hands at the spring. I could feel the cold water warring with the sunshine in her sinews. She would never have done with splashing eyelids and ears, and cheeks and red arms and throat. The rosebushes behind her leaped in the wind. The boy and his mother and the grandmother knelt at that same place and splashed after that same manner. Then the grandmother nudged me.

"Wash," she said.

I washed.

We climbed into that dove-cote block-house on stilts. We ate like four plough-horses and a colt. We consumed corn-bread and fat pork, then corn-bread and beans, then corn-bread and butter. I ate supper, breakfast, and dinner in three quarters of an hour.

III

A Brief Siesta

Working a farm of fields that stand on edge, without men to help, and without much machinery, makes women into warriors or kills them. The grandmother and mother were no longer women. Even when they caressed the boy their faces were furrowed with invincible will-power. But Lady Iron-Heels still a woman, was confused in the alternative of manhood or death. She was indeed a flower not yet torn to pieces by the wind, greatly shaken, and therefore blooming the faster.

There was a red ribbon streaming over the gray rag-carpet. Lady Iron-Heels stooped, gave the ribbon a jerk, and a banjo came snarling from under the bed.

She sat on the warring colors of the crazy-quilt, and played a dance-tune, storming the floor with one heel. She grew pensive. She sang : —

> "We shall rest in the fair and happy land
> Just across on the ever-green shore,
> Sing the song of Moses and the Lamb (by and by)
> And dwell with Jesus evermore."

Her neck had a yellow handkerchief round it. A brown lock swept across her leaping throat. Her cheeks and chin were bold as her iron heels. Underneath the precious silken sunburn, the blood was beating, beating, and trying to thicken into manhood to fight off death.

After the music the ladies dipped snuff in the circle around the dim fire.

IV

"THAT'S ALL THE CHURCH I GET"

I made a great palaver to Iron-Heels about giving me the banjo ribbon. She consented easily. Coquetry was not her specialty.

"What might be your name?" she asked.

There was no dodging now. The old woman spoke up as though to save me pain: "His name is Nicholas. But he is no kin to Lawyer Nicholas of Flagpond."

After a long silence the girl said: "We came from Flagpond, once upon a time."

She had been looking out the door at the clear bowl of the spring, and the reflection of the tall bushes, leaping in the wind.

I thought to myself: "She herself was John Kenton's chief rose." I thought: "He had her in mind when he set these ameliorating bushes through the wild." Possibly the girl could not read or write. Yet she was royal.

Democracy has the ways of a jackdaw. Democracy hides jewels in the ash-heap. Democracy is infinitely whimsical. Every once in a while a changeling appears, not like any of the people around, a changeling whose real ancestors are aristocratic souls forgotten for centuries. As the girl's eyes narrowed, she became Queen Thi, the masterful and beautiful potentate of immemorial Egypt whose face I have seen in a museum, carved on a Canopic jar. She was Queen Thi only an instant, then she became a Tennessee girl again, with the eyes of a weary doe.

She said: "Them roses give me comfort. That's all the church I get."

I asked: "Why are there so many roses between here and Greenville and none near Flag-pond?"

It was her turn not to speak. The old woman as though to save her pain, answered: "The flowers of these parts were all brought in by

John Kenton. He lived in Flagpond, but could not sell them there."

And the mother of the little boy, the man-woman, whose husband had killed Kenton, broke her long silence: "The only flowers we have to-day are these he brought. I think we would die without them. . . . How do we get through the winter?"

Lady Iron-Heels and her sister-in-law took a swig of whisky from the jug under the table, and lifted up their hoes from the floor. The boy whimpered for a drink. They said: "Wait till you are a man." All three climbed the hill.

Lady Iron-Heels was the last to go over the ridge. She saw me gather buds from both those bushes by the spring. She made a gesture of salute with her hoe.

I never travelled that way again. I passed by quickly; therefore I had a glimpse of what she was intended to be. "He that loseth his life shall find it." I see her many a time when I am looking on scattered rose-leaves. She was a woman, God's chief rose for man. She was scorned and downtrodden, but radiant still. I am only saying that she wore the face of Beauty when Beauty rises above circumstance.

The buds that I had gathered did not fall to pieces till I had passed by Daniel Boone's old trail on through Cumberland Gap, on over big hill Kentucky into the Blue Grass. On the way I wrote this, their poor memorial, the Canticle of the Rose : —

It is an article of my creed that the petals of this flower of which we speak are a medicine, that they can almost heal a mortal wound.

The rose is so young of face and line, she appears so casually and humbly, we forget she is an ancient physician.

Yet so much tradition is wrapped around her stalk, it is strange she is not a mummy. Her ashes can be found in the tombs of the Pharaohs, in everlasting companionship with the ashes of the lotus and the papyrus plant. Her dust travels on every desert wind.

No love-song can do without her.

No soldier and no priest can scorn her. There were the Wars of the Roses. And there was a Rose in Sharon. Our wandering brother Dante found a great rose in Paradise.

There are white roses, sweet ghosts under the pine. There are yellow roses, little suns in the shadow. But the normal bloom is red, flushed with foolish ardors, laughing, shaking off the gossamer years. She remembers Love, but not too well, if love is pain. There is no yesterday that can daunt her and keep her dear heart-laughter down. In springtime her magic petals bring God to the weary and give Heaven's strength to the wavering of heart.

She can turn the slave to a woman, the woman to something a little more than mortal. Oh, how bravely, with the same life-giving red, with the last of her virgin strength, she blooms and blooms on almost every highway. We find her on the road to Benares, on the road to Mecca, on the road to Rome, and on the road to Nowhere, in Tennessee.

Her red petals can almost heal a mortal wound.

II

A MENDICANT PILGRIMAGE IN THE EAST

IN LOST JERUSALEM

BEHOLD the Pharisees, proud, rich, and damned,
Boasting themselves in lost Jerusalem,
Gathered a weeping woman to condemn,
Then watching curiously, without a sound
The God of Mercy, writing on the ground.
How looked his sunburned face beneath the sun
Flushed with his Father's mighty angel-wine?
God make us all divine.

A TEMPLE MADE WITH HANDS

I

The Dwelling-place of Faith, Hope, and Charity

I HAD walked twelve miles before noon. Then I had eaten four slices of bread and butter on merciful doorsteps. At four-thirty, having completed twenty-one miles, I entered the richest village in the United States, a village that is located in New Jersey. I was so weary I was ready to sleep in the gutter, and did not care if the wagons ran over me. I should have walked through to the green fields before I looked for hospitality. I knew that the well-meant deeds of the city cannot equal the kindness of the most commonplace farm-hand. Yet I lingered.

I purchased a feast of beefsteak and onions at an obscure Jewish restaurant and felt myself once more a man. But it was now too late to leave town. The rule of the country is — one must ask for his night's lodging before five o'clock. After that, things are growing dark, and people may be afraid of you.

After paying for beefsteak and onions, I had twenty-five cents. This twenty-five cents was all that remained after a winter's lecturing on art and poetry in Manhattan. I am satisfied that the extra money, over and above all paid debts, brought me some of the ill-luck of the night. As I have before observed, money is a hoodoo on the road. Until a man is penniless he is not stripped for action.

A sign at the lunch-counter advertised: "Furnished rooms, fifty cents."

I asked the proprietor to cut the price. He dodged the issue. "Say, why don't you go up there to the mission? They will sell you a good bed cheap."

"For a quarter?"

"Something like that."

"Show me the place."

As of old the Jew pointed out the way of salvation. The Gentile followed it and reached the dwelling-place of Faith, Hope, and Charity.

"What do you want?" The questioner, evidently in charge of the place, was accoutred

in stage laboring-man style. Maybe his para-
phernalia was intended to put him on a level
with wayfarers. He wore a slouch hat, a soft
shirt, and no necktie. His clothes had the store
freshness still. They looked rather presumptu-
ous in that neat, well-stocked reading room.

"I want a cheap bed."

"We do not sell beds."

"I was told you did."

"We give them away."

"All right."

"But you have to work."

"Very well."

"Do you want to leave early in the morning?"
(The place was evidently a half-way house for
tramps.)

"Yes. I want to leave early in the morning."

"Then you will have to split kindling two
hours to-night."

"Show me the kindling."

II

SPLITTING KINDLING

In the basement I throned myself on one
block while I chopped kindling on another.

Before me, piled to the first story, was a cellarful
of wood, the record of my predecessors in toil.
I gathered that the corporal's guard of the un-
employed who stayed at the mission that night,
and had been there two or three days, had
finished their day's assignment of splitting.
They completely surrounded me, questioned
me with the greatest curiosity, and put me
down as a terrific liar, for I answered every
question with simple truth.

As soon as the melodramatic workingman-boss
went up stairs, one of them said, "Don't work
so fast. It's only a matter of form this late at
night. They want to see if you are willing,
that's all."

I chopped a little faster for this advice. Not
that I was out of humor with the advisers, —
though I should have been, for they were box-
car tramps.

One of them, having an evil and a witty eye,
said, "If I was goin' west like you, I'd start
about ten o'clock to-night and be near Buffalo
before morning."

Another, a mild nobody, professed himself a
miller. He told what a wonderful trick it was
to say, "Leddy, I'm too tired to work till I eat,"
and after eating, to walk away.

The next, a carriage painter of battered gentility, told endless stories of the sprees that had destroyed him. Another, a white frog with a bald head and gray mustache, quite won my heart. He said, "Wait till you get a nice warm bath after service. Then you'll sleep good."

To my weary and addled brain the mission was like one of those beautiful resting-places in Pilgrim's Progress. It became my religion, just to split kindling. I failed to apprehend what infinitesimal nobodies these fellows around me were. I should have disliked them more.

The modern tramp is not a tramp, he is a speed-maniac. Being unable to afford luxuries, he must still be near something mechanical and hasty, so he uses a dirty box-car to whirl from one railroad-yard to another. He has no destination but the cinder-pile by the water-tank. The landscape hurrying by in one indistinguishable mass and the roaring of the car-wheels in his ears are the ends of life to him. He is no back-to-nature crank. He is a most highly specialized modern man. All to keep going, he risks disease from these religious missions, from foul box-cars, and foul comrades. He risks accident every hour. He is always liable to the cruelty of conductor or brakeman and to murder by companions.

He runs fewer risks in the country, yet his aversion to the country is profound. He knows all that I know about country hospitality, that it can be purchased by the merest grain of courtesy. Yet most of the farm-people that entertained me had not seen a tramp for months.

To account for some of the happenings of this tale I will only add that a speed-maniac at either end of the social scale is not necessarily a hustler, personally. But in one way or another he is sure to be shallow and artificial, the grotesque, nervous victim of machinery. And a "Mission," an institution built by speed-maniacs who use automobiles for speed-maniacs who use box-cars, is bound to be absurd beyond words to tell it.

III

THE SERMON ON THE MOUNT

I loved all men that night, even the fellow in melodramatic laboring-man costume, who appeared after two hours to drive us animals up stairs into one corner of the chapel, where a dozen of our kind had already assembled from somewhere.

On the far side of that chapel sat the money-fed. The aisle was a great gulf between them and us. I smiled across the gulf indulgently, imagining by what exhortations to "Come and help us in our problem" those uncomfortable persons had been assembled. An unmitigated clergyman rose to read a text.

I presume this clergyman imagined Christ wore a white tie and was on a salary promptly paid by some of our oldest families. But I share with the followers of St. Francis the vision of Christ as a man of the open road, improvident as the sparrow. I share with the followers of Tolstoi the opinion that when Christ proclaimed those uncomfortable social doctrines, he meant what he said.

The clergyman read: "Blessed are the poor in spirit, for theirs is the kingdom of heaven."

"Blessed are they that mourn, for they shall be comforted."

"Blessed are the meek, for they shall inherit the earth."

He read much more than I will quote. Here is the final passage: —

"Ye have heard how it hath been said : 'An eye for an eye and a tooth for a tooth.' But I say unto you that you resist not evil. But whosoever shall smite thee on thy right cheek, turn to him the other also. And if any man will sue thee at the law, and take away thy coat, let him have thy cloak also. And whosoever shall compel thee to go a mile, go with him twain. Give to him that asketh thee, and to him that would borrow of thee, turn not thou away."

This Pharisee smugly assumed that he was authorized by the Deity to explain away this scripture. And he did it, as the reader has heard it done many a time.

The Pharisee was followed by a fat Scribe who tried to smile away what the other fellow had tried to argue away. The fat one then called on the assembly to bow, and exhorted the repentant to hold up their hands to be prayed for.

I held up my hand. Was I not eating the bread of the mission? And then I felt like a sinner anyway.

"Thank God," said the fat one.

After a hymn, testimonies were called for. I felt the spirit move me, but some one had the floor. Across the gulf she stood, an exceedingly

well-dressed and blindly devout sister. She
glanced with a terrified shrinking at the animals
she hoped to benefit. She said: —

"There has been one great difficulty in my
Christian life. It came with seeking for the
Spirit. Sometimes we think it has come with
power, when we are simply stirred by our own
selfish desires. Our works will show whether
we are moved by the Spirit."

I wanted to preach them a sermon on St.
Francis. But how could I? There was still
a quarter in my own pocket. Meanwhile there
rose a saint with a pompadour and blocky jaws.
He was distinctly inferior in social position to a
great part of the saints. It was probable he
had given that testimony many times. But
he did not want the meeting to drag. He spake
in a loud voice: "I was saved from a drunkard's life, in this mission, eighteen years ago,
and ever since, not by my own power, but by
the grace of God, I have been leading a God-
fearing and money-making life in this town."
That was his exact phrase, "a money-making
life." His intention was good, but he should
have been more tactful. The Pharisee looked
annoyed.

IV

A Screaming Farce

I advise all self-respecting citizens to skip this section. It is nothing but over-strained, shabby farce.

The throng melted. Scribe and Pharisee, Dives, Mrs. Dives, and their satellites went home to their comfortable beds. Many of the roughs on our side of the house found somewhere else to stay. The fellow dressed like a workingman in a melodrama sought the consolations of his own home. Had the last authority departed? Were we to have anarchy? The Frog, in his gentlest manner, sidled up to make friends again.

"Now you can have your nice warm bath, you two." I looked around. There were two of us then. Beside me, fresh from a box-car was a battered scalawag. The Frog must have let him in at the last moment.

We three climbed to the bath-room.

"Wait a minute," said the Amphibian. He disappeared. I opened my eyes, for this creature spake with a voice of authority. The box-car scalawag grinned sheepishly.

There was a scuffling overhead, a scratch and a rumble. We two looked up just in time to dodge the astonishing vision of a clothes-horse descending through a trap-door by a rope. At the upper end of the rope was the absurd bald head of our newly achieved superintendent.

"Hello, Santy Claus," said the box-car tramp. "Whose Christmas present is this?"

The Frog shouted: "Put your shoes and hats in the corner. If you have any tobacco, put it in your shoes. Hang everything else on the clothes-horse."

I obeyed, except that I had no tobacco. The rascal by my side had a plenty, and sawdusted the bath-room floor with some of it, and the remainder went into his foot-gear. Then we two, companions in nakedness, watched the Frog haul up our clothes out of sight. He closed the trap-door with many grunts.

Then this Amphibian, this boss, descended and entered the bath-room. He was a dry-land Amphibian. He had never taken a bath himself, but was there to superintend. He seemed to feel himself the accredited representative of all the good people behind the mission, and no doubt he was.

"Can it be possible," I asked myself, "that they have chosen this creature to apply their Christianity?"

The Frog said to my companion: "Git in the tub."

Then he turned on the water, regulated the temperature, and watched as though he expected one of us to steal the faucets from the wash-bowl. He threw a gruesome rag at the tramp, and allowed him to scrub himself. The creature bathing seemed well-disposed toward the idea, and had put soap on about one-third of his person when the Frog shouted: "I've got to get up at four-thirty."

The scalawag took the hint and rose like Venus from the foam. He splashed off part of it, and rubbed off the rest with a towel that was a fallen sister of the wash-rag.

The Frog was evidently trying to enforce, in a literal way, regulations he did not understand. He wiped out the bath-tub most carefully with the unclean wash-rag. Then he provided the scalawag with a shirt for night-wear. The creature put it on and said: —

"Ain't I a peach?"

He was.

The nightie was an old, heavily-starched dress-shirt, once white. Maybe it had once been worn by the Scribe or the Pharisee. But it had not been washed since. The rascal cut quite a figure as he took long steps down the corridor to bed, piloted by the hurrying Amphibian. He was a long-legged rascal, and the slivered remainders of that ancient shirt flapped about him gloriously.

I was hustled into the tub after the rascal. I was supervised after the same manner. "Now wash," boomed the Amphibian. He threw at me the sloppy rag of my predecessor.

I threw it promptly on the floor.

"I don't use a wash-rag," I said.

"Hurry," croaked the Frog. *And he let the water out of the tub.* He handed me the towel the scalawag had used. I had not, as a matter of fact, had a bath, and I was quite footsore.

"I do not want that towel," I said.

"You're awful fancy, aren't you?" sneered the Frog.

Wherever I was damp, I rubbed myself dry with my bare hands, being skilled in the matter, meanwhile reflecting that there is nothing worse than a Pharisee except a creature like this. I wondered if it was too late to rouse a mob among the better element of the town, neither saints nor sinners, but just plain malefactors of great wealth, and have this person lynched. There were probably multi-millionnaires in this town giving ten-dollar bills to this mission, who were imagining they were giving a free bath to somebody.

I wanted to appeal to some man with manicured hands who had grown decently rich robbing the widow and the orphan and who now had the leisure to surround himself with the appurtenances of civility and the manners of a Chesterfield.

"I am through with the poor but honest submerged tenth. Rich worldlings for mine," I muttered.

"Put these on," squeaked the Frog. His manner said, "See how good we are to you." He held out the treasure of the establishment, a night-garment retained for fastidious newarrivals, newly-bathed. Of course, no one else was supposed to bathe.

Was the garment he held out a slivered shirt? Nay, nay. It was a sort of pajama combination. Hundreds of men had found shelter, taken a luxurious bath, and put them on. They were companions in crime of the towel and the wash-rag. Let us suppose that three hundred and sixty-five men wore them a year. In ten years there would have been about three thousand six hundred and fifty bathed men in them. That did not account for their appearance.

"What makes them so dirty?" I asked.

No answer.

"Can't I wear my underclothes to bed instead of these?"

"No."

"Why?"

"Sulphur."

"What do you mean by sulphur?"

"Your clothes are up stairs being fumigated."

"Can't I get my socks to-night? I always wash them before I go to bed."

"No. It's against the law of the state. And you would dirty up these bowls. I have just scrubbed them out."

"I will wash them out afterward."

"I haven't time to wait. I must get up at four-thirty."

"But why fumigate my clean underwear, and give me dirty pajamas?"

K

The Frog was getting flabbergasted. "I tell you it's the law of New Jersey. You are getting awful fancy. If I had had my way, you would never have been let in here."

"Blessed are the meek, for they shall inherit the earth," I said to myself, and put on the pajamas.

This insanitary director showed me my bed. It was in a long low room with all the windows closed, where half a score were asleep. The sheets had never, never, never been washed. Why was it that in a mission so shiny in its reading room, and so devout in its chapel, so melodramatic with its clean workman-boss, in the daytime, these things were so?

The lights went out. I kicked off the pajamas and slept. I awoke at midnight and reflected on all these matters. I quoted another scripture to myself: "I was naked, and ye clothed me."

V

The Highway of Our God

At six o'clock I was called for breakfast. My sulphur-smelling clothes were on my bed.

I put them on with a light heart, for after all I had slept well, and my feet were not stiff. The quarter was still in my trousers' pocket. I presume that hoodoo quarter had something to do with the bad breakfast.

The Amphibian was now cook. He gave each man a soup-plate heaped with oat-meal. If it had been oats, it would have been food for so many horses. Had the Frog been up since four thirty preparing this?

The price of part of that horse-feed might have gone into something to eat. There was a salty blue sauce on it that was called milk. And there was dry bread to be had, without butter, and as much bad coffee as a man could drink.

A person called the bookkeeper arrived with the janitor. I made my formal farewells to those representatives of the law, before whom the Amphibian melted with humility. The scalawag who had bathed with me tipped me a wink, and tried to escape in my company. But I bade him good-by so firmly that the authorities noticed, and the brash creature remained glued to his chair. He probably had to do his full share of kindling before he escaped.

I went forth from that place into the highway of our God, who dwelleth not in temples made with hands, neither is worshipped with men's hands, as though He needed anything, seeing He giveth to all men life and breath and all things.

I said in my heart: "I shall walk on and on and find a better, a far holier shrine than this at the ends of the infinite earth."

THE TOWN OF AMERICAN VISIONS

(Springfield, Illinois)

Is it for naught that where the tired crowds see
Only a place for trade, a teeming square,
Doors of high portent open unto me
Carved with great eagles, and with hawthorns
    rare?

Doors I proclaim, for there are rooms forgot
Ripened through æons by the good and wise:
Walls set with Art's own pearl and amethyst
Angel-wrought hangings there, and heaven-hued
    dyes:—

Dazzling the eye of faith, the hope-filled heart:
Rooms rich in records of old deeds sublime:
Books that hold garnered harvests of far lands,
Pictures that tableau Man's triumphant climb:

Statues so white, so counterfeiting life,
Bronze so ennobled, so with glory fraught
That the tired eyes must weep with joy to see
And the tired mind in Beauty's net be caught.

Come enter there, and meet To-morrow's Man,
Communing with him softly day by day.
Ah, the deep vistas he reveals, the dream
Of angel-bands in infinite array —

Bright angel-bands, that dance in paths of earth
When our despairs are gone, long overpast —
When men and maidens give fair hearts to Christ
And white streets flame in righteous peace at
    last.

ON BEING ENTERTAINED ONE EVEN-
ING BY COLLEGE BOYS

I walked across the bridge from New Jersey into Easton, Pennsylvania, one afternoon. I discovered there was a college atop of the hill. In exchange for a lecture on twenty-six great men [1] based on a poem on the same theme, that I carried with me, the boys entertained me that night. They did not pay much attention to the lecture. Immediately before and after was a yell carnival. There was to be a game next day. They were cheering the team and the coach with elaborate reiteration. All was astir.

But for all this the boys spoke to me gently, gave me the privileges of the table, the bath-room, the dormitory. The president of the Y. M. C. A. lent me a clean suit of pajamas. He and two other young fellows delighted my

[1] Portions of this poem are scattered through this book for interludes. Others are already printed in *General Booth and Other Poems*.

vain soul, by keeping me up late reciting all the poems I knew.

I record these things for the sake of recording one thing more, the extraordinary impression of buoyancy that came from that school. It was inspiring to a degree, a draught of the gods. Coming into that place not far from the centre of hard-faced Easton-town I realized for the first time what sheltered, nurtured boy-America was like, and what wonders may lie beneath the roofs of our cities.

THAT WHICH MEN HAIL AS KING

WOULD I might rouse the Cæsar in you all,
(That which men hail as king, and bow them
    down)
Till you are crowned, or you refuse the crown.
Would I might wake the valor and the pride,
The eagle soul with which he soared and died,
Entering grandly then the fearful grave.
God help us build the world, like master-men,
God help us to be brave.

NEAR SHICKSHINNY

I

Leaving New Jersey I kept from all contact with money, and was consequently turning over in memory many delicious adventures among the Pennsylvania-German farmers. After crossing that lovely, lonely plateau called Pocono Mountain, I descended abruptly to Wilkesbarre by a length of steep automobile road called Giant Despair.

It was a Sunday noon in May. Wilkesbarre was a mixture of Sabbath calm and the smoke of torment that ascendeth forever. One passed pious faces too clean, sooty faces too restless. I hurried through, hoping for more German farmers beyond. But King Coal had conspired against the traveller, and would not let him go. The further west I walked, the thicker the squalor and slag heaps, and the presence of St. Francis seemed withdrawn from me, though I had been faithful in my fashion.

King Coal is a boaster. He says he furnishes

food for all the engines of the earth. He says he is the maker of steam. He says steam is the twentieth century. He holds that an infinite number of black holes in the ground is a blessing.

He may say what he likes, but he has not excused himself to me. He blasts the landscape. Never do human beings drink so hard to forget their sorrow as in the courtyards of this monarch. To dig in a mine makes men reckless, to own one makes them tormentors.

I had a double reason for hurrying on. My rules as a mendicant afoot were against cities and railroads. I flattered myself I was called and sent to the agricultural laborer.

When the land grew less black and less inhabited, I mistakenly rejoiced, assuming I should soon strike the valleys where grain is sown and garnered. Yet the King was following me still, like a great mole underground. There was no coal on the surface. The land was rusty-red and ashen-gray, — as though blasted by the torch of a Cyclops and only yesterday cooled by the rain. The best grain that could have been scattered among such rocks with the hope of a crop was a seed of dragons' teeth.

How long the desolation continued! Toward the end of the day in the midst of the nothingness, I came upon a saloon full of human creatures roaring drunk. Otherwise there was not so much as a shed in sight.

Four vilely dirty little girls came down the steps carrying beer. One of them, too intoxicated for her errand, entrusted her can to her companions. They preceded me toward the smoke-veiled sun by a highway growing black again with the foot-prints of the King.

Now there was a deafening explosion. I sat down on a rock examining myself to see if I was still alive. The children pattered on. My start seemed to amuse them immensely. I followed toward the new civil war, or whatever it was.

Just over the crest and around the corner I encountered the King's never-varying insignia, the double-row of "company houses."

Every dwelling was as eternally and uniformly damned as its neighbor, making the eyes ache, standing foursquare in the presence of the insulted daylight. Every porch and railing was jig-sawed in the same ruthless way. Every front yard was grassless. Everything was made

of wood, yet seemed made of iron, so black it
was, so long had it stood in the wasting weather,
so steadily had it resisted the dynamite now
shaking the earth.

There they stood, thirty houses to the left,
thirty to the right, with what you might call a
street between, whose ruts were seemingly cut
by the treasure-chariots of the brimstone
princes of the nether world.

Two-thirds of the way through, several
young miners were exploding giant powder.
As I approached I saw another was loading his
pistol with ball-cartridges and shooting over
the hills at the sun. He did not put it out.

The group of children with the beer served
these knights of dynamite, holding up the cans
for them to drink. The little cup-bearers were
then given pennies. They scurried home.

By their eyes and queer speech I guessed that
these children were Poles, or of some other race
from Eastern Europe. I guessed the same
about the men celebrating. Every porch on
both sides of that street held some heavy headed
creatures from presumably the same foreign
parts. They were, no doubt, good citizens
after their peculiar fashion, but with counte-

nances that I could not read. Though the next explosion seemed to jolt the earth out of its orbit, they merely blinked.

I said to myself, "This is not the fourth of July. Therefore it must be the anniversary of the day when 'Freedom shrieked' and 'Kosciuszko fell.'"

I reached the end of the street; nothing beyond but a hollow of hills and a dubious river, enclosing a new Tophet, that I learned afterwards was Shickshinny. It was late. I wanted to get beyond to the green fields.

I zigzagged across that end of the street to folk on the front porches that I thought were Americans. Each time I vainly attempted conversation with some dumb John Sobieski in Sunday clothes. I wondered what were the Polish words for bread, shelter, and dead broke.

II

THE SON OF KING COAL

Some spick and span people came out on the porch of the last house. Possibly they could understand English. I went closer. They were out and out Americans.

So I looked them in the eye and said: "I would like to have you entertain me to-night. I am a sort of begging preacher. I do not take money, only food and lodging."

"A beggin' preacher?"

"My sermon is in poetry. I can read it to you after supper, if that will suit."

"What sort of poetry?" asked the man.

"I can only say it is my own."

"Why I just LOVE poetry," said the woman. "Come in."

"Come up," said the man, and hustled out a chair.

"I'll go right in and get supper," said the wife. She was a breezy creature with a loud musical voice. She doubtless developed it by trying to talk against giant powder.

I told the man my story, in brief.

After quite a smoke, he said, "So you've walked from Wilkesbarre this afternoon. Why, man, that's seventeen miles."

I do not believe it was over fourteen.

He continued, "I'm awful glad to see a white man. This place is full of Bohunks, and Slavs, and Rooshians, and Poles and Lickerishes (Lithuanians?). They're not bad to have

around, but they ain't Cawcasians. They all
talk Eyetalian."

The fellow's manner breathed not only race-
fraternity, but industrial fraternity. It had
no suggestion of sheltered agricultural caution.
It was sophisticated and anti-capitalistic. It
said, "You and I are against the system.
That's enough for brotherhood."

Now that he stood and refilled his pipe from a
tobacco box nailed just inside the door, I saw
him as in a picture-frame. He had powerful
but slanting shoulders. He was so tall he must
needs stoop to avoid the lintel. With his bent
neck, he looked as though he could hold up a
mine caving in. His general outlines seemed
to be hewn from fence-rails, then hung with
grotesque muscles of loose leather. His eye-
brows were grown together. From looking
down long passageways his eyes were marvel-
lously owl-like. He was cadaverous. He had
a beak nose. He had a retreating chin but,
breaking the rules of phrenology, he managed
to convey the impression of a driving personal-
ity. He looked like an enormous pickaxe.

He calmly commented: "Them Polacks
waste powder awful. Not only on Sunday, for

fun, but down in the mine they use twice too much. And they can't blast the hardest coal, either. . . . And they're always gettin' careless and blowin' themselves to hell and everybody else. It's awful, it's awful," he said, but in a most philosophic tone.

He lowered his voice and pointed with his pipe stem: "Them people that live in the next house are supposed to be Cawcasians, but they haven't a marriage license. They let their little girl go for beer this afternoon, for them fellows explodin' powder over there. 'Taint no way to raise a child. That child's mother was a well-behaved Methodist till she married a Polack, and had four children, and he died, and they died, and some say she poisoned them all. Now she's got this child by this no-account white man. They live without a license, like birds. Yet they eat off weddin's."

"Eat off weddings?"

"Yes," he said. "These Bohunks and Lickerishes all have one kind of a wedding. It lasts three days and everybody comes. The best man is king. He bosses the plates."

"Bosses the plates?"

"Yes. They buy a lot of cheap plates.

L

Every man that comes must break a plate with a dollar. The plate is put in the middle of the floor. He stands over it and bangs the dollar down. If he breaks the plate he gets to kiss and hug the bride. If he doesn't break it, the young couple get that dollar. He must keep on givin' them dollars in this way till he breaks the plate. Eats and plates and beer cost about fifty dollars. The young folks clear about two hundred dollars to start life on."

"And," he continued, "the folks next door make a practice of eatin' round at weddin's without puttin' down their dollars."

I began to feel guilty.

"It's a good deal like my begging supper and breakfast of you." He hadn't meant it that way. "No," he said, "you're takin' the only way to see the country. Why, man, I used to travel like you, before I was married, except I didn't take no book nor poetry nor nothin', and wasn't afeered of box-cars the way you are. . . . I been in every state in the Union but Maine. I don't know how I kept out of there. . . . I've been nine years in this house. I don't know but what I see as much as when I was on the go. . . .

"That fellow Gallic over there that was shootin' that pistol at the sky killed a man named Bothweinis last year and got off free. It was Gallic's wedding and Bothweinis brought fifty dollars and said he was goin' to break all the plates in the house. He used up twelve dollars. He broke seven plates and kissed the bride seven times. Then the bride got drunk. She was only fifteen years old. She hunted up Bothweinis and kissed him and cried, and Gallic chased him down towards Shickshinny and tripped him up, and shot him in the mouth and in the eye. . . . The bride didn't know no better. . . . He was an awful sight when they brought him in. The bride was only a kid. These Bohunk women never learn no sense anyway. They're not smart like Cawcasian women, and they fade in the face quick."

He reflected: "My wife's a wonderful woman. I have been with her nine years, and she learns me something every day, and she still looks good in her Sunday clothes."

He became lighter in tone again. "What these Bohunks need is a priest and a church to make them behave. They mind a priest some,

if he is a good priest.   They're all Catholics, or
no church. . . ."

"Seems though sometimes a man's GOT to
shoot.   Some of them devils over there used to
throw rocks at my door, but one Sunday I
filled 'em full of buckshot and they quit.   The
justice upheld me.   I didn't have to pay no
fine.   They've been pretty good neighbors since,
pretty good neighbors."

There was a sound as though the flagstones of
eternity had been ripped up.   He saw I didn't
like it and said consolingly, "They'll stop and
go to supper pretty soon.   They eat too much
to do anything but set, afterwards.   They don't
have nothin' to eat in the old country but raw
turnips.   Here they stuff themselves like toads.
I don't see how they save money the way they
do.   The mine owners squeeze the very life out
of 'em and they wallow in beer.   I've always
made big money, but somehow never kept it.
Me and my wife are spenders.   But I ain't
afraid, for I am the only man on the street that
can dig the hardest coal.   I could dig my way
out of hell with my pick, and by G—— once
I did it, too."

The wife came to the door newly decked in an

elaborate lace waist, torn, alas, at the shoulder. Husband was right. She looked good. She announced radiantly: "Come to supper."

Then she rushed down between the houses and shouted: "Jimmy and Frank, come here! What you doin'? Get down off that roof. What you doin', associatin' with them Polack children? What you doin' with them switches?" Then she swore heartily, as unto the Lord, and continued, "They're helpin' them Polack kids switch that poor little drunk American child. Come down off that coal shed!"

They slunk into sight. She snatched their switches from them.

"Who started it?"

Jimmy admitted he started it. He looked capable of starting most anything, good or bad. He had eyes like black diamonds, a stocky frame, and the tiny beginnings of his mother's voice.

"I don't know whether to lick you or not," she said judicially. Finally: "Go up to bed without supper."

Jimmy went.

She addressed us in perfect good humor, as a musical volcano might: "Come and eat."

III

THE DAUGHTER OF THE KING

Never did I see beefsteak so thick. There was a garnish of fried onions. There was a separate sea of gravy. There was a hill of butter, a hill of thickly sliced bread. There was a delectable mountain of potatoes. That was all. These people were living the simple life, living it in chunks.

At table, as everywhere, the husband solemnly deferred to the wife. She was to him a druid priestess. And so she was radiant, as woman enthroned is apt to be. Of course, no young lady from finishing school would have liked the way we tunnelled and blasted our way through the provender. We were gloriously hungry and our manners were a hearty confession of the fact.

My passion for the joys of the table partially sated, I began to realize the room. There were hardly any of the comforts of home. There was a big onyx time-piece, chipped, and not running. Beside it was a dollar alarm-clock in good trim.

There were in the next room, among other

things, two frail gilt parlor chairs, almost black. The curtains were streaked with soot and poorly ironed. She said she had washed them yesterday. But, she continued, "I just keep cheerful, I don't keep house. Doesn't seem like I can, this street is so awful dirty and noisy and foreign."

"Yet you like it," said the husband.

"Yes," she said, "that's because I'm half Irish. The Irish were born for excitement."

"What's *your* ancestry?" I asked the husband.

"My father was a mountain white. Moved here from North Carolina, and dug coal and married a Pennsylvania Dutch lady."

"It's your turn," she said to me. "You are a preacher?"

"That's a kind of an excuse I make."

"You can't be any worse than the preacher we had here," continued the wife. "He lived down toward Shickshinny. He preached in an old chapel. He wouldn't start a Sunday school. We needed one bad enough. He just married folks. He hardly ever buried them. They say he was afraid. And," she continued, with a growing tone of condemnation, "it's a preacher's BUSINESS to face death.

"Just about the time two of our children died of diphtheria, was when he came to these parts. He was a Presbyterian, and I was raised a Presbyterian, and he wouldn't preach the funeral of my two babies. He promised to come, and we waited two hours. So I just read the Bible at the grave."

This she recounted with a bitter sense of insult.

"And the same day he locked up his mother, too."

"Locked up his mother?"

"Yes. Some said he wanted to visit a woman he didn't want her to know about. They said he was afraid she would follow him and spy. He locked up the old lady, and she about yelled the roof off, and the neighbors let her out.

"And then," continued my hostess, "when he was dying, he sent for a Wilkebsarre priest."

"Sent for a priest?" I exclaimed, completely mystified.

"Yes," she whispered. "He must have been a Catholic all the time. And the priest wouldn't come either. *That's what that old preacher got for being so mean.*"

She continued: "That preacher wasn't much meaner than the man is in the company store."

She was bristling again.

"He won't deliver goods up here unless you run a big bill. If I want anything much while big Frank here is at work, I have to take Jimmy's little play express-wagon and haul it up."

And now she was telling me of her terrible fright three days ago, down at the company store, when there was a rumor of an accident in one of the far tunnels of the mine.

"All the foreign women came running down the hill, half-crazy. I am used to false alarms, but I could hardly get up to this house with my goods. I was expecting to see big Frank brought in, just like he was before little Frank was born, eight years ago."

Little Frank lifted his face from its business of eating to listen.

"The first thing that boy ever saw was his father on the floor there, covered with blood."

"You don't remember it, Frank?" asked his father, grinning.

"Nope."

The wife continued: "There was only one

doctor came. We had a time between us. The other doctor was tendin' the men husband had dug out. The coal fell on them and mashed them flat. It couldn't quite mash husband. He's too tough," she said, lovingly. "He grabbed his pick and he tunnelled his way through, with the blood squirting out of him."

Husband grinned like a petted child. He said: "It wasn't quite as bad as that, but I was bloody, all right."

She continued with a gesture of impatience: "This is cheerful Sunday night talk. Let's try something else. What kind of a poem are you goin' to read?"

"It tells boys how to be great men, but it's for fellows of from fifteen to twenty. You'll have to save it for your sons till they grow a bit."

She was at the foot of the stairway like a flash.

"Son, dress and come down to supper."

Son was down almost as soon as she was in her chair, pulling on a stocking as he came. And he was hungry. He ate while we talked on and on.

IV

The Grandsons of the King

After the supper the dishes waited. The wife said: "Now we will have the poetry." I said in my heart, "Maybe this is the one house in a hundred where the seed of these verses will be sown upon good ground."

We went into the parlor, distinguished as such by the battered organ. The mother had Frank and Jimmy sit in semicircle with her and big Frank, while I plunged into my rhymed appeal. After the dynamite of the day I did not hesitate to let loose the thunders. I did not hesitate to pause and expound: — the poem being, as I have before described, many stanzas on heroes of history, with the refrain, ever and anon: *God help us to be brave.* No, kind and flattering reader, it was NOT above their heads. Earnestness is earnestness everywhere. The whole circle grasped that I really expected something unusual of those boys with the black-diamond eyes, no matter what kind of perversity was in them at present.

I said, in so many words, as a beginning, that nitro-glycerine was not the only force in the world, that there is also that dynamite called the power of the soul, and that detonation called fame.

But I did not dwell long upon my special saints, Francis of Assisi and Buddha, nor those other favorites who some folk think contradict them: Phidias and Michael Angelo. I dwelt on the strong: Alexander, Cæsar, Mohammed, Cromwell, Napoleon, and especially upon the lawgivers, Confucius, Moses, Justinian; and dreamed that this ungoverned strength before me, that had sprung from the loins of King Coal, might some day climb high, that these little wriggling, dirty-fisted grandsons of that monarch might yet make the world some princely reparation for his crimes.

After the reading the mother and father said solemnly, "it is a good book."

Then the wife showed the other two pieces of printed matter in the household, a volume of sermons, and a copy of *The House of a Thousand Candles*. You have read that work about the candles. The sermons were by the Reverend Wood M. Smithers. You do not know the Reverend Mister Smithers? He has collected in one fair volume all the sermons that ever put you to sleep, an anthology of all those discourses that are just alike.

She said she had read them over and over again to the family. I believed it. There was butter on the page. I said in my heart: "She is not to be baffled by any phraseology. If she can get a kernel out of Wood M. Smithers, she will also derive strength from my rhyme."

She promised she would have each of the boys pick out one of the twenty-six great men for a model, as soon as they were schooled enough to choose. She put the poem in the kitchen table drawer, where she kept some photographs of close relatives, and I had the final evidence that I had become an integral part of the family tradition.

V

ON TO SHICKSHINNY

They sent me up to bed. I put out the lamp at once, lest I should see too much. I went to sleep quickly. I was as quickly awakened. Being a man of strategies and divertisements, I reached through the blackness to the lamp that was covered with leaked oil. I rubbed this on my hands, and thence, thinly over my whole body. Coal oil too thick makes blisters; thin enough, brings peace.

I remember breakfast as a thing apart. Although the table held only what we had for supper, warmed over, although the morning light was grey, and the room the worse for the grey light, the thing I cannot help remembering was the stillness and tenderness of that time. Father and mother spoke in subdued human voices. They had not yet had occasion to shout against the alarums and excursions of the day. And the sensitive faces of the boys, and the half-demon, half-angel light of their eyes stirred me with marvelling and reverence for the curious, protean ways of God.

And now I was walking down the steeps of Avernus into Shickshinny, toward the smoke of torment that ascends forever. Underfoot was spread the same dark leprosy that yesterday had stunted flower and fruit and grass-blade.

I hated King Coal still, but not so much as of yore.

WHAT THE SEXTON SAID

Your dust will be upon the wind
Within some certain years,
Though you be sealed in lead to-day
Amid the country's tears.

When this idyllic churchyard
Becomes the heart of town,
The place to build garage or inn,
They'll throw your tombstone down.

Your name so dim, so long outworn,
Your bones so near to earth,
Your sturdy kindred dead and gone,
How should men know your worth?

So read upon the runic moon
Man's epitaph, deep-writ.
It says the world is one great grave.
For names it cares no whit.

It tells the folk to live in peace,
And still, in peace, to die.
At least, so speaks the moon to me,
The tombstone of the sky.

DEATH, THE DEVIL, AND HUMAN KINDNESS

The Shred of an Allegory

I

The Undertaker

Curious are the agencies that throw the true believer into the occult state. Convalescence may do it. Acts of piety may do it. Self-mortification may do it.

After reading my evening sermon in rhyme in the house of the stranger, I had slept on the lounge in the parlor. The lounge had lost some of its excelsior, and the springs wound their way upwards like steel serpents. So strenuous had been the day I could have slumbered peacefully on a Hindu bed of spikes.

I awoke refreshed, despite several honorable scars. What is more important I left that house with faculties of discernment.

I did not realize at first that I was particu-

larly spiritualized. I was merely walking west,
hoping to take in Oil City on my route. Yet I
saw straight through the bark of a big maple,
and beheld the loveliest . . . but I have not
time to tell.

Then I heard a fluttering in a patch of tall
weeds and discovered what the people in fairy-
land call . . . but no matter. We must hurry
on.

At noon your servant was on the front step
of a store near a cross-roads called Cranberry,
Pennsylvania. The store was on the south
side of the way by which I had come. I sat
looking along wagon tracks leading north,
little suspecting I should take that route soon.

On one side overhead was the sign: "Fred
James, Undertaker." On the other: "Fred
James, Grocer."

"And so," I thought, *"I am going to meet,
face to face, one of the eternal powers.* He may
call himself Fred James all he pleases. His
real name is Death."

I met the lady Life, once upon a time, long
ago. She had innocent blue eyes. Alone in
the field I felt free to kiss the palm of her
little hand, under the shadow of the corn.

M

It has nothing to do with the tale, but let us here reflect how the corn-stalk is a proud thing, how it flourishes its dangerous blades, guarding the young ear. It will cut you on the forehead if the wind is high. Above the blades is the sacred tassel like a flame.

Once, under that tassel, under those dangerous blades, I met Life, and for good reason, bade her good-by. After her solemn words of parting, she called me back, and mischievously fed me, from the pocket of her gingham apron, crab apples and cranberries. Ever since that time those fruits have been bitter delights to my superstitious fancy.

And here I was at CRANBERRY cross-roads, with a funeral director's sign over my head. A long five minutes I meditated on the mystery of Life and Death and cranberries. A fat chicken, apparently meditating on the same mystery, kept walking up and down, catching gnats.

At length it was revealed to me that when things have their proper rhythm Life and Death are interwoven, like willows plaited for a basket. Somewhat later in the afternoon I speculated that when times are out of joint, it is because Death reigns without Life for a partner, with the assistance of the Devil rather. But do not remember this. It anticipates the plot.

One does not hasten into the presence of the undertaker. One rather waits. HE was coming. I did not look round. Even at noon he cast a considerable shadow.

The shadow dwindled as he sat on the same step and asked: "What road have you come?" His non-partisan drawl was the result, we will suppose, of not knowing which side of the store the new customer approached.

"I came from over there. I have been walking since sunrise."

He had some account of my adventures, and my point of view as a religious mendicant. I knew I would have to ask the further road of him, but disliked the necessity. He waited patiently while I watched my friend, the fat chicken, explore an empty, dirty, bottomless basket for flies.

"I want to go west by way of Oil City," I finally said.

He answered: "Oil City is reached by the north road, straight in front of you as you sit.

It is about an hour's walk to the edge of it. It is a sort of trap in the mountains. When you get in sight of it, *keep on going down.*" This he said very solemnly.

He put his hand on my shoulder: "Come in and rest and eat first. It won't cost you a cent."

I was hungry enough to eat a coffin handle, and so I looked at him and extended my hand. He was a handsome chap, with a grey mustache. His black coat was buttoned high. He was extra neat for a country merchant, and chewed his tobacco surreptitiously. His face was not so bony and stern as you might think.

I gave him an odd copy of the *Tree of Laughing Bells*, still remaining by me. He looked at the outside long, doing the cover more than justice. Then he opened it, with a certain air of delicate appreciation. I urged him to postpone reading the thing till I was gone.

His store was high and long and narrow and cool. There was a counter to the west, a counter to the east. Behind the western one were tall coffin cupboards. As he proudly opened and shut them, one could not but notice the length of his fingers and their dexterity. He showed plain coffins and splendid coffins. He unscrewed the lid of one, that I might see the silky cushions within. They looked easier than last night's lounge.

As he stepped across what might be called the international date line of the store, and entered the hemisphere of groceries, he began to look as though he would indulge in a merry quip. A faint flush came to his white countenance, that shone among the multi-colored packages.

Before us were the supplies of a rural general store, from the kitchen mop to the blue parlor vase. Hanging from the ceiling was an array of the flamboyant varnished posters of the seedsmen, with pictures of cut watermelons, blood-red, and portraits of beets, cabbages, pumpkins.

I read his home-made sign aloud: "I guarantee every seed in the store. Pansy seeds a specialty."

"Not that they all grow," he explained. "But the guarantee keeps up the confidence of the customers. I have made more off of vegetable and flower seeds this year than caskets."

He pulled out a chip plate and fed me with dried beef, sliced thin.

He smiled broadly, and set down a jar. The merry quip had arrived.

"Why," he asked, "is a stick of candy like a race-horse?"

I remained silent, but looked anxious to know. Delighted with himself, he gave the ancient answer, and with it several sticks of candy. Kind reader, if you do not know the answer to the riddle, ask your neighbor.

There was no end of sweets. He skilfully sliced fresh bread, and spread it with butter and thick honey-comb. With much self-approval he insisted on crowding my pockets with supper.

"Nobody knows how they will treat you around Oil City. *I go often, but never for pleasure. Only on funeral business.*"

He gave me pocketfuls of the little animal crackers, so daintily cut out, that used to delight all of us as children. Since he insisted I take something more, I took figs and dates.

He held up an animal cracker, shaped like a cow, and asked: "When was beefsteak the highest?" I ventured to give the answer.

Death is not a bad fellow. Let no man cross his grey front stoop with misgiving. The honey he serves is made by noble bees. Yet do not go seeking him out. No doubt his acquaintance is most worth while when it is casual, unexpected, one of the natural accidents. And he does not always ask such simple riddles.

II

THE TRAP WITHOUT THE BAIT

It was about two o'clock when the north road left the cornfields and reached the hill crests above the city. How the highway descended over cliffs and retraced itself on ridges and wound into hollows to get to the streets! At the foot of the first incline I met a lame cat creeping, panic-stricken, out of town.

Oil City is an ugly, confused kind of place. There are thousands like it in the United States.

I reached the post-office at last. *There was no letter for me at the general delivery. I was expecting a missive.* And now my blistered heels, and my breaking the rule to avoid the towns, and my detour of half a day were all in vain.

Oil City, in her better suburbs, as a collection of worthy families in comfortable homes, may have much to say for herself. But as a corporate soul she has no excuse. The dominant, shoddy architecture is as eloquent as the red nose of a drunkard. I do not need to take pains to work her into my allegory. The name she has chosen makes her a symbol. No doubt others reach the very heart of her only to find it empty as the post-office was to me. Baffling as this may be, there is another risk. Escape is not easy.

Almost out of town at last, I sat down by the fence, determined not to stir till morning. I said, "I can sleep with my back against this post."

I had just overtaken the lame cat, and she now moved past me over the ridge to the cornfields. She seemed most unhappy. I looked back to that oil metropolis. *I wondered how many had lived and died there when they would have preferred some other place.*

III

A Mysterious Driver

A fat Italian came by in a heavily-tired wagon. The wagon was loaded with green bananas. The fruit-vendor stopped and looked me over. He most demonstratively offered me a seat beside him. He had a Benvenuto Cellini leer. He wore one gold earring. He looked like the social secretary of the Black Hand.

He was apparently driving on into the country. Therefore I suffered myself to be pulled up on to the seat. Around the corner we came to green fields and bushes, and I thanked the good St. Francis and all his holy company.

I said to my charioteer: "As soon as you get a mile out, let me down. I do not want to get near any more towns for awhile."

"Allaright," he said. On his wrist was tattooed a blue dagger. The first thing he did was unmerciful. He went a yard out of his way to drive over the lame cat which had stopped in despair, just ahead of us. Pussy died without a shriek. Then the cruel one, gathering by my manner that I was not pleased with this incident, created a diversion. He reproved his horse for not hurrying. It was not so much a curse as an Italian oration. The poor animal tried to respond, but hobbled so, his master surprised me by checking the gait to a walk. Then he cooed to the horse like a two hundred pound turtledove.

In a previous incarnation this driver must have been one of the lower animals, he had so many dealings with such. Some rocks half the size of base-balls were piled at his feet. A ferocious dog shot out from a cottage doorway. With lightning action he hurled the ammunition at the offender. The beast retreated weeping aloud from pain. And Mr. Cellini showed his teeth with delight.

And now, after passing several pleasant farm-houses, where I ran a chance for a free lodging for the asking, I was vexed to be suddenly driven into a town. We hobbled, rattled on, into a wilderness thicker every minute with fire-spouting smoke-stacks.

"This ees Franklin," said my charioteer. "Nice-a-town. *MY* town," he added earnestly. "I getta reech (rich) to-morrow."

He began to cross-examine the writer of this tale. I counselled myself not to give my name and address, lest I be held for ransom.

After many harmless inquiries, he asked in a would-be ingratiating manner, "Poppa reech?"

"No. Poor."

"Poppa verra reech?"

"No. Awfully poor. But happy and contented."

"Where your Poppa leeve?"

"My father is the Man in the Moon."

That answer changed him completely. I seemed to have given the password. I had joined whatever it was he belonged to. He gave me three oranges as a sign.

I had hoped we would drive past the smoke and fire. But he turned at right angles, into the midst of it, and drove into a big black barn. He waved me good-by in the courtliest manner, as though he were somebody important, and I were somebody important.

Pretty soon I asked a passer-by the nearest way to the suburbs. I had to walk on the edges of my feet they were so tired. The street he pointed out to me was nothing but a continuation of tar-black, coughing, out-of-door ovens, side by side, shoulder to shoulder, on to the crack of doom. I presume, in the language of this vain world, they were coke ovens.

I opened my eyes as little as possible and breathed hardly at all. Then, by way of diversion, I nibbled animal crackers, first a dog, then a giraffe, then a hippopotamus, then an elephant.

Those ovens looked queerer as the street led on. There were subtle essences abroad when the smoke cleared away, and when the great roar ceased there were vague sounds that struck awe into the heart. I may be mistaken, but I think I know the odor of a burning ghost on the late afternoon wind, and the puffing noise he makes.

As the cinders crunched, crunched, underfoot, the conviction deepened: "These ovens are not mere works of man. Dying sinners snared and corrupted by Oil City are carried here when the city has done its work — carried in the wagon of Apollyon, under bunches of green bananas. Body and soul they are disintegrated by the venomous oil; they crumble away in the town of oil, and here in the town of ovens, the fragments are burned with unquenchable fire."

Now it was seven o'clock. The street led
south past the aristocratic suburbs of Franklin,
and on to the fields and dandelion-starred
roadside.

IV

The Allegory Breaks Down. My Friend
Humankindness with the Green Galluses

I hoped for a farm-hand's house. Only in
that sort will they give free lodging so near
town. And, friends, I found it, there on the
edge of the second cornfield. The welcome was
unhesitating.

I looked at my host aghast. To satisfy my
sense of the formal, he should have had the
dignity to make him Father Adam, and lord of
Paradise. How could one round out a day that
began loftily with Death, and continued gloriously with some one mighty like the Devil,
with this inglorious type now before me? He
wrecked my allegory. There is no climax in
Stupidity.

Just as the colorless, one-room house had
stove, chimney, cupboard, adequate roof, floor,
and walls, so the owner had the simplified,

anatomical, and phrenological make-up of a man. He had a luke-warm hand-clasp. He smoked a Pittsburg stogy. He had thick vague features and a shock of drab hair. The nearest to a symbol about him was his new green galluses. I suppose they indicated I was out in the fields again.

If his name was not Stupidity, it was Awkwardness. He kept a sick geranium in an old tomato can in the window. He had not cut off the bent-back cover of the can. Just after he gave me a seat he scratched his hand, as he was watering the flower, and swore softly.

Yet one must not abuse his host. I hasten to acknowledge his generous hospitality. If it be not indelicate to mention it, he boiled much water, and properly diluted it with cold, that the traveller might bathe. The bath was accomplished out of doors beneath the shades of evening.

Later he was making preparations for supper, with dull eyes that looked nowhere. He made sure I fitted my chair. He put an old comfort over it. It was well. The chair was not naturally comfortable; it was partly a box.

After much fumbling about, he brought some baked potatoes from the oven. The plate was so hot he dropped it, but so thick it would not break.

He picked up the potatoes, as good as ever, and broke some open for me, spreading them with tolerable butter, and handing them across the table. Then I started to eat.

"Wait a minute," he said. He bowed his head, closed his dull eyes, and uttered these words: "The Lord make us truly thankful for what we are about to receive. Amen."

I have been reproved by some of the judicious for putting so much food in these narratives. Nevertheless the first warm potato tasted like peacocks' tongues, the next like venison, and the next like ambrosia, and the next like a good warm potato with butter on it. One might as well leave Juliet out of Verona as food like this out of a road-story. As we ate we hinted to each other of our many ups and downs. He mumbled along, telling his tale. He did not care whether he heard mine or not.

He had been born near by. In early manhood he had been taken with the oil fever. It happened in this wise: — He had cut his foot splitting kindling. Meditating ambition as he slowly recovered, he resolved to go to town. He sold his small farm and wasted his substance in speculation. At the same time his young wife and only child died of typhoid fever. He was a laborer awhile in the two cities to the northeast. Then he came back here to plough corn.

He had been saving for two years, had made money enough to go back "pretty soon" and enter what he considered a sure-thing scheme, that I gathered had a close relation to the oil business. He said that he had learned from experience to sift the good from the bad in that realm of commerce.

He put brakes on the slow freight train of his narrative. "I was about to explain, when you ast to come in, that I don't afford dessert to my meals often."

"If you will excuse me," I said, emptying my pockets, "these figs, these dates, these oranges, these animal crackers were given me by Death, and the Devil. Eat hearty."

"Death and the Devil. What kind are they?"

"They're not a bad sort. Death gave me

honey for dinner, and the Devil did no worse than drive me a little out of my way."

He smiled vaguely. He thought it was a joke, and was too interested in the food itself to ask any more questions.

The balmy smokeless wind from the south was whistling, whistling past the window, and through the field. How much one can understand by mere whispers! The wind cried, "Life, life, life!" Some of the young corn was brushing the walls of the cottage, and armies on armies of young corn were bivouacing further down the road, lifting their sacred tassels toward the stars.

There was no change in the expression of the countenance of my host, eating, talking, or sitting still in the presence of the night. I may have had too poor an estimate of his powers, but I preached no sermon that evening.

But, like many a primitive man I have met, he preached me a sermon. He had no bed. He gave the traveller a place to sleep in one corner and himself slept in the opposite corner. The floor was smooth and clean and white, and the many scraps of rag carpet and the clean comfort over me were a part of the sermon.

N

Another part was in his question before he slept:
"Does the air from that open window bother
you?"

I assured him I wanted all there was, though
from the edge of the world.

He had awkwardly folded his new overcoat,
and put it under my head. . . . And so I
was beginning to change his name from Stupidity and Awkwardness to Humankindness.

Though in five minutes he was snoring like
Sousa's band, I could not but sleep. When I
awoke the sun was in my eyes. It shone
through the open door. Mr. Humankindness
was up. The smell of baked potatoes was in
the air. Outside, rustled the corn. The wind
cried, "Life, life, life."

LIFE TRANSCENDENT

This being the name of praise given to a fair lady.

I USED to think, when the corn was blowing,
Of my lost lady, *Life Transcendent,*
Of her valiant way, of her pride resplendent:
For the corn swayed round, like her warrior-
    band
When I knelt by the blades to kiss her hand.
But now the green of the corn is going,
And winter comes and a springtime sowing
Of other grain, on the plains we knew.
So I walk on air, where the clouds are blowing,
And kiss her hand, where the gods are sowing
Stars for corn, in the star-fields new.

IN THE IMMACULATE CONCEPTION CHURCH

HUNTED by friends who think that life is play,
Shaken by holy loves, more feared than foes,
By beauty's amber cup, that overflows,
And pride of place, that leads me more astray :—

Here I renew my vows, and this chief vow —
To seek each year this shrine of deathless power,
Keeping my springtime cornland thoughts in
    flower,
While labor-gnarled grey Christians round me
    bow.

Arm me against great towns, strong spirits old!
St. Francis keep me road-worn, music-fed.
Help me to look upon the poor-house bed
As a most fitting death, more dear than gold.

Help me to seek the sunburned groups afield,
The iron folk, the pioneers free-born.

Make me to voice the tall men in the corn.
Let boyhood's wildflower days a bright fruit
    yield.

Scourge me, a slave that brings unhallowed
    praise
To you, stern Virgin in this church so sweet,
If I desert the ways wherein my feet
Were set by Heaven, in prenatal days.

THE OLD GENTLEMAN WITH THE LANTERN (AND THE PEOPLE OF HIS HOUSEHOLD)

I

THE SAVAGE NECKLACE

THE reader need not expect this book to contain any nicely adjusted plot with a villain, hero, lawyer, papers, surprise, and happy ending. The highway is irrelevant. The highway is slipshod. The highway is as the necklace of a gipsy or an Indian, a savage string of pebbles and precious stones, no two alike, with an occasional trumpery suspender button or peach seed. Every diamond is in the rough.

I was walking between rugged farms on the edge of the oil country in western Pennsylvania.

The road, almost dry after several days of rain, was gay with butterfly-haunted puddles. The grotesque swain who gave me a lift in his automobile for a mile is worth a page, but we will only say that his photograph would have contributed to the gaiety of nations — that he

was the carved peach-stone on the necklace of
the day.

There was a complacent cat in a doorway,
that should have been named "scrambled eggs
and milk," so mongrel was his overcoat. There
was a philosophic grasshopper reading inscrip-
tions in a lonely cemetery, with whom I had a
long and silent interchange of spirit. Even the
graveyard was full of sun.

On and on led the merry morning. At
length came noon, and a meal given with hearti-
ness, as easily plucked as a red apple. For half
an hour after dinner in that big farm-house we
sat and talked religion.

O pagan in the cities, the brand of one's belief
is still important in the hayfield. I was delighted to discover this household held by conviction to the brotherhood of which I was still
a nominal member. Their lingo was a taste
of home. "Our People," "Our Plea," "The
pious unimmersed." Thus did they lead themselves into paths of solemnity.

Then, in the last five minutes of my stay, I
gave them my poem-sermon. The pamphlet
made them stare, if it did not make them think.

Splendor after splendor rolled in upon the

highway from the four corners of heaven. Why then should I complain, if about four o'clock the prosy old world emerged again?

The wagon-track now followed a section of the Pennsylvania railroad, and railroads are anathema in my eyes when I am afoot. There appeared no promising way of escape. And now the steel rails led into a region where there had been rain, even this morning. More than once I had to take to the ties to go on. When the mud was at all passable I walked in it by preference, fortifying myself with these philosophizings : —

"Cinders are sterile. They blast man and nature, but the black earth renews all. Mud upon the shoes is not a contamination but a sign of progress, eloquent as sweat upon the brow. Who knows but the feet are the roots of a man? Who knows but rain on the road may help him to grow? Maybe the stature and breadth of farmers is due to their walking behind the plough in the damp soil. Only an aviator or a bird has a right to spurn the ground. All the rest of us must furrow our way. Thus will our cores be enriched, thus will we give fruit after our kind."

Whistling pretty hard, I made my way. And now I had to choose between my rule to flee from the railroad, and my rule to ask for hospitality before dark.

At length I said to myself: "I want to get into a big unsophisticated house, the kind that is removed from this railroad. I want to find an unprejudiced host who will listen with an open mind, and let me talk him to death."

To keep this resolve I had to hang on till near eight o'clock. The cloudy night made the way dim. At length I came to a road that had been so often graded and dragged it shed water like a turtle's shell. It crossed the railway at right angles and ploughed north. I followed it a mile, shaking the heaviest mud from my shoes. Led by the light of a lantern, I approached a dim grey farm-house and what would have been in the daytime a red barn.

II

BY THE LIGHT OF THE LANTERN

The lantern was carried, as I finally discovered, by an old man getting a basket of chips near the barn gate. He had his eye on me as I leaned over the fence. He swung the lantern closer.

"My name is Nicholas," I said. "I am a professional tramp."

"W-e-l-l," he said slowly, in question, and then in exclamation.

He flashed the lantern in my face. "Come in," he said. "Sit down."

We were together on the chip-pile. He did not ask me to split kindling, or saw wood. Few people ever do.

In appearance he was the old John G. Whittier type of educated laboring man, only more eagle-like.   He spoke to me in a kingly prophetic manner, developed, I have no doubt, by a lifetime of unquestioned predominance at prayer-meeting and at the communion table. It was the sonorous agricultural holy tone that is the particular aversion of a certain pagan type of city radical who does not understand that the meeting-house is the very rock of the agricultural social system. As far as I am concerned, if this manner be worn by a kindly old man, it inspires me with respect and delight. In a slow and gracious way he separated his syllables.

"Young man, you are per-fect-ly wel-come

to shel-ter if we are on-ly sure you will not do us an in-ju-ry. My age and ex-per-ience ought to count for a lit-tle, and I assure you that most free travel-ers abuse hos-pi-tal-ity. But wait till my daugh-ter-in-law comes."

I was shivering with weariness, and my wet feet wanted to get to a stove at once. I did not feel so much like talking some one to death as I had a while back.

By way of passing the time, the Patriarch showed me his cane. "Pre-sen-ted at the last old set-tel-ers' picnic because I have been the pres-i-dent of the old-settlers' association for ten years. Young man, why don't you carry a cane?"

"Why should I?"

"Won't it help you to keep off dogs?"

I replied, "A housekeeper, if she is in a ner-vous condition, is apt to be afraid of a walking-stick. It looks like a club. To carry something to keep off dogs is like carrying a lightning-rod to keep off lightning. I encounter a lot of barking and thunder, but have never been bitten or blasted."

And while I was thus laboring for the respect of the Patriarch, the daughter-in-law stepped into the golden circle of the lantern light. She had just come from the milking. I shall never forget those bashful gleaming eyes, peering out from the sunbonnet. Her sleeves were rolled to the shoulder. Startling indeed were those arms, as white as the foaming milk.

She set down the bucket with a big sigh of relaxation. She pushed back the sunbonnet to get a better look. The old man addressed her in an authoritative and confident way, as though she were a mere adjunct, a part of his hospitality.

"Daugh-ter, here is a good young man — he Looks like a good young man, I think a stew-dent. You see he has books in his pock-et. He wants a night's lodging. Now, if he *is* a good young man, I think we can give him the bed in the spare room, and if he is a bad young man, I think there is enough rope in the barn to hang him before day-light."

"Yes, you can stay," she said brightly. "Have you had supper?"

It is one of the obligations of the road to tell the whole truth. But in this case I lied. The woman was working too late.

"Oh yes, I've had supper," I said.

And she carried the milk into the darkness.

In the city, among people having the status indicated by the big red barn and the enormous wind-mill and a most substantial fence, this gleaming woman would have languished in shelter. She would have played at many philanthropies, or gone to many study clubs or have had many lovers. She would have been variously adventurous according to her corner of the town. Here her paramour was WORK. He still caressed her, but would some day break her on the wheel.

The old man sent me toward the front porch alone. There was a rolling back of the low gray clouds just then, and the coming of the moon. The moon's moods are so many. To-night she took the forlornness out of the restless sky. She looked domestic as the lantern.

III

YOU OUGHT TO BE ASHAMED OF YOURSELF

I was on the porch, scraping an acquaintance with the grandmother. She held a baby in her lap. They sat in the crossing of the moonlight and the lamplight.

There was no one to explain me. I explained myself. She eyed me angrily. She did not want me to shake hands with the baby. She asked concerning her daughter-in-law.

"And did she say you could stay?"

"She did."

The grandmother brought a hard fist down on the arm of the chair: "I'd like to break her neck. She's no more backbone than a rabbit."

I do not distinctly remember any bitter old man I have met in my travels. She was the third bitter old woman. Probably with the same general experiences as her husband, she had digested them differently. She was on the shelf, but made for efficiency and she was not run down.

In her youth her hair was probably red. Though she was plainly an old woman, it was the brown of middle age with only a few streaks of gray. Under her roughness there were touches of a truly cultured accent and manner. I would have said that in youth she had had what they call opportunities.

I asked: "Isn't the moon fine to-night?"

She replied: "Why don't you go to work?"

I answered: "I asked for work in the big

city till I was worn to a thread. And you are
the first person who has urged it on me since
I took to tramping. I wonder why no one
ever thought of it before."

She smiled grudgingly.

"What kind of work did you try to do in the
city?"

"I wanted to paint rainbows and gild side-
walks and blow bubbles for a living. But no
one wanted me to. It is about all I am fit for."

"Don't talk nonsense to me, young man!"

"Pardon me, leddy — I am a writer of
rhymes."

"The nation's going to the dogs," she said.
I suppose I was the principal symptom of
national decay.

Just then a happy voice called through the
house, "Come to supper."

"That's for you," said the grandmother.
"You ought to be ashamed of yourself."

IV

Gretchen-Cecilia, Waitress

I went in the direction of the voice, delighted,
not ashamed. There, in that most cleanly

kitchen, stood the white-armed milkmaid, with cheeks of geranium red. She had spread a table before me in the presence of mine enemy. I said: "I did not ask for supper. I told you I had eaten."

"Oh, I knew you were hungry. Wait on him, Gretchen-Cecilia."

My hostess scurried into the other room. She was in a glorious mood over something with which I had nothing to do.

Gretchen-Cecilia came out of the pantry and poured me a glass of warm milk. I looked at her, and my destiny was sealed forevermore — at least for an hour or so. The sight of her brought the tears to my eyes.

I know you are saying: "Beware of the man with tears in his eyes." Yes, I too have seen weeping exhibitions. I remember a certain pious exhorter. The collection followed soon. And I used to hear an actor brag about the way he wept when he looked upon a certain ladylike actress whom we all adore. He vividly pictured himself with a handkerchief to his devoted cheeks, waiting in the wings for his cue. He had belladonna eyes. At the risk of being classed with such folk, I reaffirm that I was a little weepy. I insist it was not gratitude for a sudden square meal — if truth be told, I have had many such — it was the novel Gretchen-Cecilia.

It took little conversation to show that Gretchen-Cecilia was a privileged character. She had little of the touch of the farm upon her. She was the spoiled pet of the house, and the index of their prosperity — what novelists call the third generation. She had a way of lifting her chin and shoving her fists deep into her apron pockets.

I said: "I have a fairy-tale to read to you after supper."

And she said: "I like fairy-tales." And then, redundantly: "I like stories about fairies. Fairy stories are nice."

It was no little pleasure to eat after nine hours doing without, and to dwell on beauty such as this after so many days of absence from the museums of art and the curio shops. Every time she brought me warm biscuits or refilled my tumbler, she brought me pretty thoughts as well.

She was nine years old, she told me. Her eyes were sometimes brown, sometimes violet.

o

Her mouth was half a cherry, and her chin the quintessence of elegance. Her braids were long and rich, her ribbons wide and crisp.

Maidenhood has distinct stages. The sixteenth year, when unusually ripe, is a tender prophecy. Thirteen is often the climax of astringent childhood, with its especial defiance or charm. But nine years old is my favorite season. It is spring in winter. It is sweet sixteen through walls of impregnable glass. This ripeness dates from prehistoric days, when people lived in the tops of the trees, and almost flew to and from the nests they built there, and mated much earlier than now.

As I finished eating, the mother brought the little brother into the room saying, "Gretchen-Cecilia, watch the baby." Then she smiled on me and said: "When she washes the dishes, you can hold him."

She had on a fresh gingham apron, blue, with white trimmings. I judged by the squeak, she had changed her shoes.

"Who's coming?" I asked, when the mother had left.

"Papa. He goes around the state and digs oil wells, and is back at the end of the week."

I was washing the dishes when Grandma came in. She frowned me away from the dishpan. She said, "Gretchen-Cecilia, wipe the dishes."

The baby howled on the floor. I was not to touch him. Gretchen-Cecilia tried to comfort him by saying, "Baby, dear dear baby; baby, dear dear baby."

"Do you realize, young man," asked Grandma, "that I, an old woman, am washing your dishes for you?"

I was busy. I was putting my wet stockinged feet on a kindling-board in the oven, and my shoes were curling up on the back of the stove.

"Young man —"

"Yessum —"

"Where's your wife?"

I replied, "I have no wife, and never did have." Then I ventured to ask, "May I have the hand of Gretchen? I want some one who can wipe dishes while I wash them."

"But I'm not grown up," piped the maiden. It seemed her only objection.

I said: "I will wait and wait till you are seventeen."

The old lady had no soul for trifles. She in-

toned, like conscience that will not be slain:
"*Where's your wife?*"

But I said in my heart: "Madam, you are
only a suspender-button upon the necklace of
the evening."

V

"Papa has Come!"

There was a scurry and a flutter. Gretchen
threw down her dish-rag, leaving Grandma a
plate to wipe.

I heard the grandfather say, "Wel-come, son,
wel-come indeed!" The young wife gave a
smothered shriek, and then in a minute I
heard her exclaim, "John, you're a scamp!"

I put on my hot shoes and went in to see
what this looked like. Gretchen-Cecilia was
somewhere between them, and then on her
father's shoulder, mussing his hair. And the
mother took Gretchen down, as John said in
reply to a question: —

"Business is good. Whether there's oil or
not, I dig the hole and get paid."

This man was now standing his full height
for his family to admire. He was one I too

could not help admiring. He had an open sunburned face, and I thought that behind it there was a non-scheming mind, that had attained good fortune beyond the lot of most of the simple. He was worth the dressing up the family had done for him, and almost worthy of Gretchen's extra crisp hair ribbons.

His wife put her arms around his neck and whispered something, evidently about me. He watched me over his shoulder as much as to say : —

"And so it's a stray dog wants shelter? No objections."

He unwrapped his package. It was an extraordinary doll, with truly truly hair, and Gretchen-Cecilia had to give him seven kisses and almost cry before he surrendered it.

He pulled off his boots and threw them in the corner, then paddled up stairs and came down in his shoes. For no reason at all Gretchen-Cecilia and her mother chased him around the kitchen table with a broom and a feather duster, and then out on to the back porch.

VI

Conferences

The grandfather called me into the front room and handed me a book.

"Yer a schol-ar. What do you think of that?"

It was a history of the county. The frontispiece was a portrait of Judge Somebody. But the book naturally opened at about the tenth page, on an atrocious engraving of this goodly old man and his not ill-looking wife. He breathed easier when I found it. It was plainly a basis of family pride. I read the inscription.

"So you two are the oldest inhabitants?" I asked.

"The oldest per-pet-ual in-habitants. I was born in this coun-ty and have nev-er left it. My wife is some young-er, but she has nev-er left it, since she married me."

Even the old lady grew civil. She tapped a brooch near her neck. "They gave me this breast-pin at the last old settlers' picnic."

The old man continued: "All the old farm is still here in our hands, but mostly rented.

It brings something, something. Our big income is from my son's well-digging. He never speculates and he makes money."

It seemed a part of the old man's pride to have even the passing stranger realize they were well-fixed. In a furtive attempt to do justice to their station in life they had a tall clock in the corner, quite new and beautiful. And, as I discovered later, there was upstairs a handsome bath-room. The rest of that new house was clean and white, but helplessly Spartan.

The old folk were called to the back porch. At the same time I heard the mother say, "Show the man your doll."

And in came the little daughter like thistle-down.

We were in that white room at opposite ends of the long table, and nothing but the immaculate cloth stretching between us. She sat with the doll clutched to her breast, looking straight into my eyes, the doll staring at me also. The girl was such a piece of bewitchment that the poem I brought to her about the magical *Tree of Laughing Bells* seemed tame to me, and everyday. That foolish rhyme was soon read and put into her hands. It seemed to give her an infinite respect for me. And any human creature loves to be respected.

On the back porch the talking grew louder.

"Papa is telling them he wants to rent the rest of the farm and move us all to town," explained Gretchen.

It was the soft voice of the young wife we heard: "Of course it will be nice to be nearer my church."

And then the young father's voice: "And I don't want Gretchen to grow up on the farm."

And the old man's voice, still nobly intoned: "And as I say, I don't want to be stub-born, but I don't want to cross the coun-ty line."

Gretchen banged the door on them and we crossed the county line indeed. We told each other fairy-tales while the unheeded murmur of debate went on.

When it came Gretchen's turn, she alternated Grimm, and Hans Andersen and the legends of the Roman Church. I had left the railroad resolved to talk some one to death, and now with all my heart I was listening. She knew the tales I had considered my special discoveries in youth: "The Amber Witch,"

"The Enchanted Horse," "The Two Brothers."
She also knew that most pious narrative, *Elsie
Dinsmore*. She approved when I told her I
had found it not only sad but helpful in my
spiritual life. She had found it just so in hers.

VII

THE SPARE ROOM

With her eyes still flashing from argument,
the grandmother took me up stairs. She gave
me a big bath-towel, and showed me the bath-
room, and also my sleeping place. I asked her
about the holy pictures hanging near my bed.
She explained in a voice that endeavored not
to censure: "My daughter-in-law is of German-
Catholic descent, and she is *still* Catholic."

"What is *your* denomination?" I asked.

"My husband and son and I are Congrega-
tionalists."

She did not ask it of me, but I said: "I am
what is sometimes disrespectfully called a
'Campbellite.'"

But the old lady was gone.

After a boiling bath I lay musing under
those holy pictures. My brother of the road,

when they put you in the best room, as they
sometimes do, and you look at the white coun-
terpane and the white sheets and the cosey
appointments, do you take these brutally, or
do you think long upon the intrinsic generosity
of God and man?

I have laid hold of hospitality coldly and
greedily in my time, but this night at least, I
was thankful. And as I turned my head in a
new direction I was thankful most of all for
the unexpected presence of the Mother of God.
There was her silvery statue near the foot of
my bed, the moonlight pouring straight in
upon it through the wide window. It spoke to
me of peace and virginity.

And I thought how many times in Babylon
I had gone into the one ever open church to
look on the crowned image of the Star of the
Sea. Though I am no servitor of Rome I
have only adoration for virginity, be it carved
in motionless stone, or in marble that breathes
and sings.

A long long time I lay awake while the image
glimmered and glowed. The clock downstairs
would strike its shrill bell, and in my heart a
censer swung.

VIII

MORNING

There was a pounding on the door and a shout. It was the young husband's voice. "It's time to feed your face."

They were at the breakfast-table when I came down. My cherished memory of the group is the picture of them with bowed heads, the grandfather, with hand upraised, saying grace. It was ornate, and by no means brief. It was rich with authority. I wanted to call in all the mocking pagans of the nation, to be subdued before that devotion. I wanted to say: "Behold, little people, some great hearts still pray."

I stood in the door and made shift to bow my head. Yet my head was not so much bowed but I could see Gretchen-Cecilia and her mother timidly cross themselves. In my heart I said "Amen" to the old man's prayer. But I love every kind of devotion, so I crossed myself in the Virgin's name.

The tale had as well end here as anywhere. On the road there are endless beginnings and few conclusions. For instance I gathered from the conversation at the breakfast table they were not sure whether they would move to the city or not. They were for the most part silent and serene.

There were pleasant farewells a little later. Gretchen-Cecilia, when the others were not looking, gave me, at my earnest solicitation, a tiny curl from the head of her doll that had truly truly hair.

I walked on and on, toward the ends of the infinite earth, though I had found this noble temple, this shrine not altogether made with hands. I again consecrated my soul to the august and Protean Creator, maker of all religions, dweller in all clean temples, master of the perpetual road.

THAT MEN MIGHT SEE AGAIN THE ANGEL–THRONG

WOULD we were blind with Milton, and we sang
With him of uttermost Heaven in a new song,
That men might see again the angel-throng,
And newborn hopes, true to this age would rise,
Pictures to make men weep for paradise,
All glorious things beyond the defeated grave.
God smite us blind, and give us bolder wings;
God help us to be brave.

Printed in the United States of America.

THE following pages contain advertisements of books by the same author.

DATE DUE

12/7/07	